A Source Book of Military Wheeled Vehicles

D1381471

Maudslay of World War I

DAF of the 1950s

A Source Book of
Military Wheeled Vehicles

Compiled by the Olyslager Organisation
Edited by Bart H. Vanderveen

WARD LOCK LIMITED · LONDON

© Olyslager Organisation and
B. H. Vanderveen

ISBN 0 7063 1285 6

First published in Great Britain 1972
by Ward Lock Limited, 116 Baker Street,
London, W1M 2 BB
Reprinted 1976

All Rights Reserved. No part of this publication
may be reproduced, stored in a retrieval system,
or transmitted, in any form or by any means,
electronic, mechanical, photocopying, recording,
or otherwise, without the prior permission of the
Copyright owners.

Text in Univers (689)

Filmset and printed in England by
Cox and Wyman Ltd,
London, Fakenham and Reading

HERTFORDSHIRE
COUNTY LIBRARY
7024228
623·747

There was a time when military vehicles were looked upon as instruments of war and few civilians took an interest in them unless they happened to own and operate an 'ex-Government' vehicle.

In recent years, however, a growing segment of the public seems to have become more aware of two aspects of military cars and trucks. Firstly their historic value, in particular the World War I and II types and, secondly, the fact that from a technical point of view military designs are often more interesting than the conventional civilian vehicles.

To automobile historians and enthusiasts, military vehicles have long seemed somewhat mysterious, mainly perhaps because so little has been known or published about them and, indeed, in many automobile history books they are virtually ignored.

This book has been compiled with the aim of familiarizing the reader with some definitions and presenting him with a pictorial history showing typical examples of cars, trucks and tractors which we, too, prefer to see operated by Defence Ministries rather than War Departments but which we feel should be given the historical and technical attention they deserve.

Restoring, preserving and running World War II transport has become a new pastime. In a BBC radio interview not long ago one of the leading British preservationists of Allied army trucks commented: 'They are easier to keep and maintain than vintage Bentleys, and let's face it, we owe such a lot to them!'.

Piet Olyslager MSAI, MSAE, KIVI

Glossary

This Source Book gives general and technical details of a wide range of typical wheeled military vehicles as produced during this century. The majority are production vehicles but some experimental and limited-production models are included. The technical data section is arranged as follows:

Engine: Number and configuration of cylinders, fuel, power output and cubic capacity. To convert cubic capacity from litres to cubic inches, multiply by 61.

Transmission: Number of forward speeds of main gearbox (there is always one reverse speed, unless stated otherwise) and, where applicable, the number of speeds of the transfer case or auxiliary gearbox. Thus, a 'four-speed with two-speed transfer' transmission has, in effect eight forward and two reverse speeds, etc.

Chassis: Usually 'ladder type' frame, which indicates two longitudinal frame side members with a number of cross members; these members may be 'I', 'channel' or 'box' section or tubular. 'Integral construction' indicates that frame or subframe(s) and body or hull are welded together to form one unit, although in certain cases the body or hull is self-supporting with the suspension bolted directly to it. Suspension is usually of the semi-elliptic leaf spring type; in such cases it is given as 'leaf spring suspension'. Any deviations are stated. Leaf spring suspension 'inverted on rear bogie' indicates that the semi-elliptical (if not 'straight') leaf spring is mounted upside down with the outer ends resting on or attached to the two rear axles and the centre fixed to the chassis frame, usually pivoting on a trunnion.

Body: Under this heading brief details about cab and/or bodywork may be found. 'Half doors' are solid (rather than canvas) doors up to waist level, with detachable upper section.

Dimensions: The first two dimensions are the overall length and width of the vehicle, where available. They are followed by the wheelbase (distance(s) between front and rear or front, middle and rear wheel centres). 'Mean' wheelbase is to centre of rear bogie. All dimensions are given in the units which are generally used in the country where the vehicle was manufactured.

Conversions:
1 metre (1 m) = 39.37 in = 3.28 ft.
1 foot (1 ft) = 12 in = 0·3 m.
1 inch (1 in) = 0·0254 m (2·54 cm).

Introduction

The term 'military vehicles' covers practically any means of land transport used by the armed forces, from bicycles to heavy armoured fighting vehicles. It also includes trailers and even sledges.

'Military MOTOR vehicles' is a more specific classification, covering self-propelled vehicles, including 'soft-skin' transport and armoured fighting vehicles. The following sub-grouping includes most types:

(1) Commercial 'off-the-shelf' vehicles, which in their standard form are suitable for a large number of military applications. Sometimes these are known as 'administrative vehicles'. In peacetime a large proportion of transport vehicles (such as motorcycles, cars, vans, trucks, buses, etc.) is included in this category, mainly for economic reasons. They lack off-road mobility and military effectiveness, but compared with the more sophisticated military tactical vehicles they are considerably cheaper to procure and maintain. During World War II many such vehicles saw active

Typical 'administrative' vehicle: $2\frac{1}{2}$-ton 4×2 cargo truck (American Ford 600)

service, some having been impressed, others because they were easier and quicker to produce than real tactical types. During World War I, of course, most military cars and trucks differed but little from their civilian counterparts. In addition to being painted in military livery these commercial

Typical 'quasi-military' vehicle: $1\frac{1}{2}$-ton 4×4 truck (German Daimler-Benz 'Unimog' S)

types are usually 'militarized' to some extent by fitting certain standardized items of equipment. Bodywork in the case of trucks in this category is often of military pattern. Sometimes oversize tyres are fitted.

(2) Commercial cross-country and special purpose vehicles originally designed for civilian use but which, in their basic form, are suitable for certain special military purposes. Many are in fact designed with possible military use in mind. They are also known as 'quasi-military' vehicles and in the case of trucks they are often adaptations of conventional civilian models, fitted with all-wheel drive, special tyres, etc. Such vehicles may be acquired by both military and civilian operators. Since World War II their number has grown enormously and in the smaller and less-developed countries vehicles of this group may form the nucleus of the armed forces' vehicular equipment. Certain specialist vehicles, e.g. commercial type mobile cranes, are also in this category.

Typical 'tactical' vehicle: 3-ton 6×6 truck (Dutch DAF YA-328)

(3) Special vehicles which have been designed and developed to meet specific military requirements, sometimes by the military authorities or agencies themselves but more usually by private firms under Government contracts. Manufacturers are not normally allowed to market these vehicles through normal commercial channels, but sometimes they are available to 'friendly nations'. Vehicles in this group are known as tactical vehicles and include special cross-country trucks and amphibious models. In the USA trucks in this category are sub-divided into standard tactical trucks (e.g. the $\frac{1}{4}$-ton, 4×4, M151) and hi-mobility tactical trucks (e.g. the 5-ton, 8×8, M656).

(4) AFVs — or armoured fighting vehicles — which category includes armoured cars, tanks, armoured personnel carriers (APC), self-propelled guns (SPs), etc. These may be wheeled, tracked, or half-tracked. AFVs form a class of their own and only some wheeled examples are shown in this book.

During World War I practically all military motor transport fell into Group 1. During the inter-war period the majority were in Groups 1 and 2.

World War II saw large-scale production of vehicles in Groups 3 and 4.

In the British and Commonwealth armies vehicles were classified 'A' and 'B'. 'A' vehicles were AFVs, 'B' vehicles were all remaining transport and special purpose vehicles, varying from motorcycles to heavy artillery tractors. Nowadays there is more activity in Groups 3 and 4 than ever before but there are also many more quasi-military vehicles. A good example of the latter type is the British Land-Rover — basically a commercial vehicle but acceptable by most forces as a military tactical truck.

After 'demob' military vehicles are often used by civilian operators, sometimes with extensive modifications. Some examples of these are shown and described in our companion volume *A Source Book of Commercial Vehicles*.

Early Origins

It is perhaps significant that the world's first

Some Fowler steam traction engines of the British Army Service Corps (Royal from 1918) on an exercise in the Aldershot area

self-propelled vehicle was a military gun tractor. This was, of course, the Frenchman Cugnot's three-wheeled steam artillery tractor of 1769/70. Although it was unsuccessful and never pulled a gun, it was far ahead of its time. A century later, the British steam traction engine first proved its usefulness for military purposes. The Corps of Royal Engineers acquired their first traction engine, 'Steam Sapper', in 1868 and a second in 1872. The latter, an Aveling and Porter, was the first mechanical transport vehicle used by the British on active service, in the Ashanti War (1873–74). It was sent out to Cape Coast Castle but was too heavy to operate satisfactorily on the West African tracks and its activities were eventually confined to sawing timber.

During the Franco-Prussian War, two Fowler steam traction engines were acquired by the German Government. They were used throughout the campaign, up to the siege of Paris. The Russians employed a dozen tractors in the Russo-Turkish war in 1878 and these were reported as doing their job well.

It was during the second Boer War in South Africa (1899–1902) that the British first employed mechanical transport successfully. They had twenty-one types of traction engine, including an armoured model, and several steam lorries were also used. The experiences gained in South Africa had much influence on the subsequent development of army motorization.

The first armed motor vehicles appeared in 1899. During that year the German-born British engineer, F. R. Simms, and the American Colonel (then Major), R. P. Davidson, completed their first machine-gun motor carriages, followed by more refined models during the following years.

About 1910 the military authorities of various nations, with varying degrees of faith and enthusiasm, began to acknowledge the importance of motorization in case of a future war. France and Germany held annual trials for various types of road transport machines, including trucks (with or without trailers) and tractors. In Britain the Automobile Association, in March 1909, had organized the famous 'Hastings Run'. They made an offer to the Secretary of State for War to transport a complete battalion to any coastal town that might be a possible scene of invasion. The town selected was Hastings and the exercise was carried out quite successfully. Plans had also been devised about a subvention or subsidy scheme whereby operators who would agree to buy and keep in sound mechanical order certain approved types of vehicles were paid an annual subsidy. Germany, France and Italy had similar schemes.

When war broke out, however, the belligerent powers found themselves equipped with very meagre stores of motor transport.

The Great War

Soon after the outbreak of war in August, 1914,

the BEF (British Expeditionary Force) disembarked in France taking with them some 1,200 vehicles. Of these only some eighty were owned by the Army, the rest being civilian models obtained under the Subsidy Impressment Scheme. More vehicles soon followed, including some 1,300 AEC 'B' type and Daimler London buses for troop transport. In the early days these were used in their peacetime livery. The French, too, employed motor trucks and buses, as well as some fine examples of four-wheel drive (4×4) artillery tractors, produced by Châtillon-Panhard, Latil, Renault and Schneider. A petrol-electric tractor was also produced, featuring a petrol engine with dynamo and an electric motor in each of the four wheels. The Germans employed load-carriers — often with special four-wheeled trailers — of a great variety of makes but largely the products of Daimler, Büssing, NAG and Gaggenau (Benz). Their artillery tractors were enormous steel-wheeled machines specially built for military purposes, rather than for agricultural or commercial work like the steam traction engines and (American) Holt Caterpillars as used by the British. The rear wheels of the German tractors were generally of large size, ranging up to eight feet in diameter, the proportions of rear and front wheels following steam traction engine practice. Some of them featured four-wheel drive and among their manufacturers were Büssing, Daimler, Dürkopp, Erhardt, Horch and Podeus. The British transport supplies were supplemented by large quantities of imported vehicles, mainly of American origin such as Autocar, FWD (first large-scale producers of 4×4 trucks), Jeffery/Nash, Locomobile/Riker, Packard, Peerless and Pierce-Arrow.

When the United States entered the war in 1917 they immediately started work on a standardized truck, known as the 'Liberty' and to be built by various manufacturers to a common military design. However, there was no time to wait for their delivery in sufficient numbers and large quantities of commercial types (over 200 different models) were shipped to Europe. The result of this enormous variety was that 445,000 line items of spare parts were required, 80% of which were not interchangeable. The maintenance problem was insurmountable and some 50 to 60% of the vehicles were unserviceable at any given time.

A purely military four-wheel drive truck-tractor, the 'Militor', was also developed in the USA but was too late for mass production. Some 7,600 'Liberty' Class B (3-to-5-ton) trucks did find their way to Europe, but also not until shortly before the war came to an end.

In April 1917 the US Army possessed just over 3,000 trucks; by the end of 1918 this had grown to approximately 85,000 and a further 100,000 had been scheduled for production up to July 1919 had the war continued.

The Italians had their own family of military vehicle types, produced by Fiat, Spa, Isotta-Fraschini, Itala, Züst, and others. They also supplied vehicles to the British who, moreover, obtained the entire output of the Swiss Berna factory.

The Russians relied almost entirely on imported vehicles, notably of British and American origin, Austins predominating among the former.

The Inter-war Period

If one thing had been learned during the Great War it was the urgent need for standardization of vehicles and replacement parts. But the 'war to end all wars' was now over. The German Army was forbidden redevelopment under the Treaty of Versailles and the other Governments did not like thinking about the possibility of a future war. Most of the vehicles were sold, and horse and mule regained their pre-war popularity. There were, however, military and civilian individuals on both sides of the Atlantic who stayed wide awake for new developments and they worked hard, with very little if any official government backing or encouragement.

Some very interesting new designs were developed. From France came the first light six-wheelers (Renault) and half-track vehicles (Citroën-Kégresse), both in the early 1920s. Heavier six- and eight-wheelers were developed in America by the Goodyear Tire & Rubber Company. Britain, after evaluating the Renault, developed her own family of light and medium six-wheelers with dual-drive rear bogies (6×4), and produced her first four-wheeled four-wheel drive (4×4) tractor: the 'Hathi'. Fitted with a dual-drive rear bogie a Thornycroft-built 'Hathi Mk II' became Britain's first 6×6. It was followed by 6×6 models from Scammell, FWD and Guy, and 8×8 tractors by Guy, AEC and Armstrong-Siddeley. The latter was a development of the Pavesi articulated 4×4 tractor which had originated in Italy. In France the all-wheel drive vehicle was further developed by firms like Latil and Renault. In America the Liberty truck was fitted with pneumatic tyres, and four- or six-wheel drive. FWD developed their famous Model B 4×4 further, and various manufacturers produced half-track vehicles, inspired by the Citroën-Kégresse.

During the early 1930s the American firm of Marmon-Herrington started building heavy all-wheel drive trucks and converting commercially available models, mainly Fords, to all-wheel-drive and half-track vehicles. In the Netherlands a simple but ingenious, tandem-drive rear bogie was produced by SYS (now Netam) and further developed and refined by Messrs Van der Trappen and Van Doorne (DAF). Called the 'Trado' system, it was used to militarize Chevrolet, Ford and other chassis.

Very active in England was Hungarian-born engineer Nicholas Straussler. His first military vehicle, built in 1933, was a light four-wheel-drive-and-steering Ford-engined runabout which could travel forward and reverse using all gears. It was an ingenious machine but not successful. This was followed by several light and heavy cross-country tractors. He also designed an interesting V8-engined eight-wheeled chassis, which was built, like several of his vehicles, by Manfred-Weiss in Hungary. Straussler became best known for his advanced rear-engined armoured car designs, featuring independent suspension front and rear, a number of which were built by Alvis. They set the pattern for British World War II armoured cars.

Germany experimented with several six-wheeler designs and developed a whole range of sophisticated military vehicles, all-wheel drive cars and trucks and a family of light, medium and heavy half-track vehicles for a variety of purposes. The best-developed cross-country vehicle of the inter-war period, internationally speaking, was however, the dual-drive six-wheeler (6×4).

The Second World War (Allied Powers)

When World War II commenced, relatively few real (tactical) military transport vehicles existed.

In England there were fair numbers of WD (War Department) six-wheelers, supplemented by militarized 4×2 vehicles of popular makes, and small quantities of 4×4 and 6×4 artillery tractors. However, much of this equipment was left behind at Dunkirk and lost. As a result so many new vehicles were needed that production considerations had an undue influence on design. Introduction of newly-developed tactical types could only take place in such a way as not to impede the total flow of vehicles. The 15-cwt 4×2 Infantry truck had been well developed during the late Thirties and production of these and the 30-cwt and 3-ton 6×4 types was increased without too much difficulty. Three-ton 4×4 trucks with large tyres were subsequently developed by various manufacturers and the original idea was for these to replace entirely the 3-ton 4×2 and 6×4 types but owing to production problems this never really materialized. It was also found impossible wholly to discontinue the 6×4 3-tonner because

certain specialist bodies and long loads could not be accommodated on the 4×4. The RAF, who until early 1941 had been developing their own transport, were the first with a 3-ton 4×4. This was the Crossley Q-type which was in production as early as April 1940.

Canada had harnessed its manufacturers to the production of standardized military pattern vehicles for its own forces and their developments and designs followed those of the British closely. Fewer manufacturers being involved, however, standardization was less difficult. Huge quantities of these military pattern vehicles were turned out by the Canadian Ford Motor Company and General Motors of Canada, a large proportion being supplied to Great Britain, Australia, India, and other Commonwealth countries.

During the threat of war prior to Pearl Harbor (in December 1941) the US Army had given serious consideration to the development of their transport. Their main requirements were met by four types: the famous $\frac{1}{4}$-ton 4×4 ('Jeep') command reconnaissance and general-purpose truck, the $\frac{1}{2}$- (later $\frac{3}{4}$-) ton 4×4 with a variety of bodies including the weapons carrier, the $1\frac{1}{2}$-ton 4×4 range, and the $2\frac{1}{2}$-ton 6×6 and 6×4 'Workhorse of the Army'. The $2\frac{1}{2}$-ton or light-heavy truck as a size was arrived at as being the heaviest vehicle which could be mass-produced within the existing facilities (GMC, Studebaker, Reo, IHC). Other standardized but limited-production types included 4-ton and 6-ton 6×6 trucks, prime movers, and special equipment vehicles. The Ordnance Department, which took over responsibility for development and procurement from the Quartermaster Corps in 1942, designed several additional types. Total military vehicle production in the US during the war was about 3,600,000. Of this total, 750,000 were sent to Allied nations under Lend-Lease, which was an international aid programme, initiated by the Americans.

The ubiquitous $\frac{1}{4}$-ton 4×4 'Jeep' became extremely popular in all theatres of war. It had a magnificent performance and set a very high standard in military wheeled vehicles. Well over 600,000 of them were produced by Willys-Overland and Ford from 1941–45 and after the war it was imitated by scores of auto makers.

Notable among Soviet trucks during World War II were the GAZ and the ZIS (Stalin). To supplement these, Russia received thousands of US, Canadian and British trucks under Lend-Lease.

World War II (Axis Powers)

During the thirties Germany, under Hitler, had started building a network of *Autobahnen*, which, like the military roads of the Roman empire, made possible the swift movement of troops to frontiers. Simultaneously the motor industry, in close co-operation with the *Heereswaffenamt*, developed and produced a multitude of military cross-country vehicles. These were followed in about 1937 by a family of sophisticated (and complicated) tactical vehicles, built by various manufacturers to a common specification. They were known as *Einheitstypen* (standardized types) and were intended to replace the earlier commercial and quasi-military types. The new generation consisted of light, medium, and heavy passenger cars (all 4×4, some with four-wheel steering), light diesel-engined trucks (6×6) and in addition, there was a whole range of semi-track vehicles (for trailing loads of up to 18 tons), called *Zugkraftwagen* (prime movers). Several of these standardized chassis were also used as a chassis for armoured vehicles.

Wehrmacht vehicles were designated according to bodywork and role by a *Kfz.* (motor vehicle) or *Sd.Kfz.* (special motor vehicle) number. *Sd.Kfz.* numbers were used only for *Wehrmacht* designs. *Kfz.* numbers did not apply to vehicle chassis. For example, the *Kfz. 15* was a medium passenger car with open (soft-top) body, four to five seats, a luggage compartment, and a towing attachment. This type of bodywork could be fitted either to a commercial car chassis or to a *Fahrgestell der m. E.Pkw.* (medium standardized car chassis). Later during the war it could even be on a modified captured chassis, known examples including American Chevrolet cars and British Morris-Commercial light truck chassis. A *Kfz. 12* was similar to a *Kfz. 15* but without the luggage compartment. In turn, a *Kfz. 11* resembled the *Kfz. 12* except for the towing hook.

The result of these countless variations was chaos in spare parts supply. Moreover, some of the various *Einheitstypen* proved rather unreliable in battle conditions and demanded considerable maintenance. The Volkswagen *Kübelwagen*, simplicity itself, replaced most of the light types, and the medium and heavy *E.Pkw.* were superseded by the Mercedes-Benz and Steyr 1500A (4×4), which also formed the basis for light trucks. Medium 4×4 trucks, adaptations of 4×2 commercial types, were produced by Opel ('Blitz'), Borgward, Daimler-Benz, KHD-Magirus, etc.

Many Ford, KHD, Mercedes-Benz and Opel truck chassis were fitted with track-bogies at the rear for use in Russia and became known as *Maultiere* (Mules).

Certain motor manufacturing plants in occupied countries, like Czechoslovakia and France, were engaged on producing for the *Wehrmacht* either their own designs or German special models. Skoda, for example, built the *Radschlepper Ost* (Wheeled Tractor East), designed by Porsche.

As in World War I, Italy had its own range of military vehicles, with a rather high degree of type standardization. Most of their designs, however, dated from the early- and mid-1930s.

The Japanese also developed their own motor vehicles, some of them patterned on American types, others of their own design.

Post-war Developments

After World War II the Allied Forces were left with enormous quantities of surplus vehicles. Vast numbers were sold, not only to truck-hungry civilian operators but also to friendly nations who had to rebuild their forces.

During the war the need for standardization had again become very evident. With this in mind the major nations soon started developing their next generation of tactical vehicles. For economic reasons many of these, however, were quasi-military types.

It was during the Korean conflict that the US Army introduced their first post-war family of military vehicles (M38, M37, M34, M135, etc.), although the majority of vehicles used there were still of World War II vintage. The new M-Series eventually consisted of only six basic chassis types with payloads from $\frac{1}{4}$ to 10 tons, presenting a vast reduction in types from that of World War II, when there were 18 classes of chassis, produced by an even greater number of manufacturers. The new system resulted in an important reduction in the spare parts problem. The total number of spare part line items for US Army trucks and trailers of all types in World War II was 450,000. This was reduced to 67,000, or 85% less, and only about half of these were for the military trucks.

In the United States, where progress in off-the-road transport vehicles had been greater than anywhere else, many different types were developed and tested. These included virtually all kinds of propulsion systems: wheels, tracks, roller-type tyres, giant tyres, chain-mounted flotation roller tyres, and revolving 'pontoons' with spiral (archimedian) blades.

The British also developed a new series of tactical transport vehicles, powered by standardized military Rolls-Royce engines. In recent years, however, most of these were replaced by more economical quasi-military types.

DAF in the Netherlands, FN in Belgium, Volvo in Sweden, Berliet in France, Fiat/OM in Italy, Barreiros in Spain, MAN and Daimler-Benz in Germany, Nissan and Toyota in Japan, and various other manufacturers introduced impressive ranges of military vehicles, mainly for the forces of their own countries, but also for export to other nations.

Canada discontinued its interesting range of military pattern vehicles and standardized on US types, whereas in Australia the International Harvester Company produces standardized 4×4 and 6×6 types for the Australian forces.

Various Communist countries also have impressive tactical vehicle fleets.

A multitude of military vehicle types has been developed since the war in every country with a motor industry. Practically everything has been tried and tactical vehicles must and do meet remarkably varied requirements. As for the future, further experimenting with wheels and tracks — with their advantages and their shortcomings — will always be going on. In addition to the new propulsion systems mentioned earlier, the Air Cushion Vehicle has made its appearance and this type may well be much in evidence in years to come.

1903/04
Austro-Daimler (A)
40 PS Panzerspähwagen

As early as 1903 the Österreichische Daimler Motoren Gesellschaft in Wiener-Neustadt (Austria) designed and built a four-wheel drive armoured car with a rotating turret. It was made under the direction of Paul Daimler. The car was demonstrated (with 2 mgs) at German Imperial Army manoeuvres in 1905 and at Austro-Hungarian manoeuvres in 1906, but remained in prototype stage. The driver occupied the usual position but when necessary could disappear from view by lowering his seat.

Engine: four-in-line, petrol, 40–45 bhp, 4.4 litres.
Transmission: four-speed; shaft drive to front and rear axles.
Chassis: ladder type; leaf spring suspension; steel-sheathed Arbel front wheels.
Body: armour plate hull and front end (3–4 mm); rotating dome-shaped turret; crew 4–5.
Dimensions: 4.60×1.76 m; wb 3.50 m.

1906
Panhard et Levassor/Genty (F)

This *'Auto-Mitrailleuse'* was designed by Captain Genty, a French artillery officer. It consisted of a 1904 Panhard open car with a Puteaux type Hotchkiss machine-gun which could be fixed on to one of two mounts, one situated between the front seats and the other at the rear of the body. There were two further seats in the back. It was used in various manoeuvres and in Morocco and could carry 2,000 rounds of ammunition. Similar bodywork and armament was later fitted on two Bayard-Clément cars (1908).
Engine: four-in-line, petrol, 24 bhp (modified, fitted with dual ignition).
Transmission: four-speed; chain final drive.
Chassis: ladder type; leaf spring suspension.
Body: open four-seater; rotating front passenger/gunner seat; two-gun mounts; no armour protection.

1911
Hupmobile (USA)
20

This little two-seater runabout was among the first cars produced by the Hupp Motor Car Corp. (1908–41) and was in production for several years. In 1911 one was acquired for use as a military scout car and tested by Thomas J. Dickson, Major Chaplain, US Army. Although it had '26 Infantry, US Army' painted on the bonnet, it was not an official Army vehicle and it was one of the few Hupmobile cars ever to see military service. This early 'Hup' could, however, be considered one of the earliest ancestors of the 'Jeep'.
Engine: four-in-line, petrol, 20 bhp, 2.8 litres.
Transmission: two-speed; shaft drive.
Chassis: ladder type; leaf spring suspension (transversal at rear).
Body: open two-seater.
Dimensions: approx. 128×60 in; wb 98 in.

1913
Fiat (I)
15 Ter

The Fiat 15 Ter *'Autocarro'* was in production from 1913 until 1922 and saw extensive service during the first World War, chiefly with the Italian and British forces. The British had almost 400 of these 1½-ton trucks and employed them mainly in Italy, Salonica and Mesopotamia. In addition to the truck, there were other body types also, including a 10–12-passenger bus. Together with the Model T Ford this Fiat was among the few contemporary types of trucks to have pneumatic tyres.

Engine: four-in-line, petrol, 40 bhp, 4.4 litres.
Transmission: four-speed; shaft drive.
Chassis: ladder type; leaf spring suspension; 880×120 tyres.
Body: open cab with folding top; wooden cargo body with hoops and tilt.
Dimensions: 4.54×1.74 m; wb 3.07 m.

1914
Leyland (GB)
S5X4

Among the most numerous of trucks used by the British during World War I was the War Office 'A' Subsidy type Leyland 3-tonner. Almost 6,000 were produced from 1915, almost exclusively for the Royal Flying Corps (later RAF). It is therefore usually called the 'RAF type'. The majority had 'heavy tender' bodywork (used for general aircraft servicing), others had tanker or workshop bodies or, as illustrated here, 'floats'. The latter were used to transport partly-dismantled aircraft etc. in large containers. Similar 3-ton 4×2 trucks were made by AEC, Albion, Daimler, Dennis, Thornycroft, etc.

Engine: four-in-line, petrol, 36 bhp, 6.6 litres.
Transmission: four-speed.
Chassis: ladder type; leaf spring suspension.
Bodywork: open cab with folding top; platform body.
Dimensions: approx.
27 ft 0 in × 7 ft 5 in; wb 13 ft 11 in.

1914
Jeffery (USA)
'Quad'

The Jeffery 'Quad' 2-ton 4×4 truck was produced throughout World War I. In mid-1917 Charles W. Nash took over the Jeffery firm and the truck was renamed Nash 'Quad'. Although available commercially, most were used by the US Army, USMC, the British and French Army, etc. The British used the 'Quad' with GS, Office, Stores and Workshop bodies, the French mainly as cargo and gun carriers (*portées*). In 1918 alone, Nash supplied almost 11,500 'Quads' for military use. It was co-produced by three other firms (Hudson, National and Paige). There was also an armoured version.

Engine: four-in-line, petrol (Buda), 32 bhp, 3.78 litres.

Transmission: four-speed; permanent all-wheel drive.

Chassis: ladder type; leaf spring suspension; four-wheel steer.

Bodywork: open cab; test body shown.

Dimensions: 200×74 in; wb 124 in.

1915
Tatra (ČS)
TL 2

Typical general service load carrier of World War I, having same general configuration as comparable trucks built in other countries at that time. The TL 2 was a 2-tonner, used by the Austro-Hungarian Army and its production span was from 1915 until 1923. It had a fuel tank capacity of 140 litres and could reach 35 km/h on good roads. The engine was of the overhead-camshaft type. Truck shown had rubber-saving sprung-metal 'tyres'. Note: before 1919 Tatra vehicles were known as Nesselsdorf.
Engine: four-in-line, petrol, 35 bhp, 3.55 litres.
Transmission: four-speed; shaft drive.
Chassis: ladder type; leaf spring suspension.
Body: open cab with folding top; wooden dropside body with hoops and tilt.
Dimensions: 5.38×1.80 m; wb 3.70 m.

1915
Fiat (I)
30 *Trattore*

The *'Tipo 30'* was a powerful tractor, used by the Italian Army for hauling heavy artillery pieces. A set of special chain/track devices was carried and could, when necessary, be fitted round the rear driving wheels in order to improve traction. The vehicle was of the forward-control configuration. (*'Tipo 20B'*, which was produced from 1915 to 1920, had normal control.) Wheel size was 900×160 front, 1,100×300 rear.
Engine: four-in-line, petrol, 60 bhp, 10.62 litres.
Transmission: four-speed; chain final drive.
Chassis: ladder type; leaf spring suspension.
Body: open cab with folding top; wooden main body with hoops and tilt.
Dimensions: length 6.20 m; wb 3.60 m.

1915
Austro-Daimler (A)
C-Zug

The *'C-Zug'* was designed by Porsche and was used by the Austro-Hungarian Army during 1915–18 for transporting heavy artillery, namely the 38-cm howitzer and 42-cm mortar (shown). For every artillery piece five of these tractors, each with 30–35-ton trailer, were used. The tractor, M16, had an engine-driven generator which powered electric motors in the tractor rear wheels and all eight trailer wheels. It could be used on roads or rails.
Engine: six-in-line, petrol, 150 bhp, driving 93 kW DC generator, powering wheel hub motors (early models: 120 bhp, 70 kW).
Transmission: electric (80-m cable between tractor and trailer so that trailer could cross bridges separately).
Chassis: ladder type; leaf spring suspension.
Body: open cab with half doors and folding top.
Dimensions: length 5.00 m; wb 3.25 m.

1915
Büssing (D)
A5P

Prototype for a four-wheel drive armoured car, featuring four-wheel steering and duplicate driving controls in the rear of the hull for driving backwards. It had a turret with three heavy machine-guns. The vehicle weighed $10\frac{1}{4}$ tons, fully equipped, and could reach a maximum speed of 35 km/h. Picture shows delivery of the vehicle to Duke Ernst August on 15 June 1916. In the foreground are Mr and Mrs Heinrich Büssing. Daimler produced an armoured car in the same year.

Engine: six-in-line, petrol, 90 bhp.
Transmission: five speeds forward and reverse; shaft drive.
Chassis: ladder type; leaf spring suspension.
Body: hull of armour plate (5–7 mm) with turret.
Dimensions: 9.50×2.10 m.

1916
Ford (USA/GB)
Model T

Several versions of the legendary
Ford Model T, popularly known as
'Tin Lizzy', saw active service in World
War I, mainly, it would appear, with
British and Commonwealth troops.
Bodywork included passenger, ambulance, van, light truck, etc. Some were
fitted with flanged wheels and acted
as 'railway trolley' on narrow-gauge
tracks. The 'T' was particularly popular
in the Middle-East (Mesopotamia,
Palestine). The British alone, by the
end of the war, had 18,984 Fords in
their inventory, about two thirds of
which were overseas.
Engine: four-in-line, petrol,
20 bhp, 2.89 litres.
Transmission: two-speed pedal-
operated planetary type.
Chassis: ladder type; transversal
leaf spring suspension.
Body: open reconnaissance/patrol
car with Vickers machine-gun.
Dimensions: approx.
11 ft 4 in × 5 ft 7 in; wb 8 ft 4 in.

1916
Berna (CH)
C2

During the First World War civilian trucks were pressed into military service. In several countries there was a subsidy or subvention scheme whereby the owners received a subsidy in return for which they had to put their vehicle at the Army's disposal should they need it. This 1½-ton Berna was requisitioned during World War I and again in World War II. It survived and was extensively restored to original condition during 1967–69.

Engine: four-in-line, petrol, 28 bhp, 5.55 litres.
Transmission: four-speed; shaft drive.
Chassis: ladder type; leaf spring suspension; fitted with sprag (hill holder).
Body: open cab with folding top; wooden dropside body.
Dimensions: 5.35×1.78 m; wb 3.50 m.

1917
Selden, etc. (USA)
Class B 'Liberty'

The US War Department in 1917 issued specifications for a standardized truck chassis in the 'A' ($1\frac{1}{2}$–2-ton) and 'B' (3–5-ton) class. The standardized 'A' did not materialize, but of the 'B', 43,000 of which were ordered from twenty-nine different manufacturers, almost 10,000 were completed by November 1918 when the war ended. These had been produced by fifteen truck makers, principally Selden, Gramm-Bernstein, Garford, Pierce-Arrow and Republic. Being a 'nationally assembled' truck it was named 'Liberty'. On the radiator it had the letters USA.

Engine: four-in-line, petrol (3 mfrs), 52 bhp, 6.96 litres.
Transmission: four-speed; worm-drive final drive.
Chassis: ladder type; leaf spring suspension.
Body: open cab with folding top; wooden body with hoops and tilt.
Dimensions: 261 × 84 in; wb $160\frac{1}{2}$ in.

1917
FWD (USA)
Model B

The famous FWD Model B 3-ton 4×4 was introduced in 1912 when the US Army tested one. Large quantities were made during 1914–18. The first large orders were placed by the British Government. Others went to Russia and France. About 16,000 were built and after the war many saw service on roadbuilding and similar jobs. They were also built in England and by three other companies in the USA (Mitchell, Premier and Kissel). Body types were numerous.
Engine: four-in-line, petrol (Wisconsin), 36 bhp, 6.37 litres.
Transmission: three-speed with single-speed transfer; permanent all-wheel drive (lockable third diff. in transfer case).
Chassis: ladder type; leaf spring suspension.
Body: open cab; searchlight on elevating platform for US Army Engineers.
Dimensions: approx: 222×71 in; wb 124 in.

1917
Krupp-Daimler (D)
KDI 46/100 PS

German four-wheel drive tractor, used for artillery towing and similar duties (*Artillerie-Kraft-Zugmaschine mit Vierradantrieb*). It was equipped with a powerful engine-driven winch and was later designated *Sd.Kfz.2 (Sonder-Kraftfahrzeug* – special motor vehicle). It was used until well into the 1930s. A special balloon-winch version and a gun-mount vehicle (SP) also existed. The tractor weighed 7,400 kg (fully equipped) and its payload (ammunition, etc.) was 2,000 kg.
Engine: four-in-line, petrol, 100 bhp, 12 litres.
Transmission: four-speed with high and low range (8F2R).
Chassis: ladder type with drop in centre; leaf spring suspension.
Body: closed cab with half-doors and side curtains; composite wood/metal main body with equipment lockers.
Dimensions: 6.40×2.20 m; wb 3.75 m.

1918
Sinclair (USA)
TTH 'Militor' M1918

In 1918 the US Ordnance Department issued a specification for a four-wheel drive truck chassis to replace the commercial 4×4 FWD and Nash 'Quad'. The Sinclair Motor Corp. of New York City was contracted but by the war's end only 150 had been completed and production stopped. At least three body styles were fitted, namely cargo, artillery tractor and ammunition carrier; the latter type is shown.
Engine: four-in-line, petrol (Wisconsin), 36.1 bhp, 6.16 litres.
Transmission: four-speed with auxiliary gearbox.
Chassis: ladder type; leaf spring suspension.
Body: open cab with folding top; special steel body with fixed sides and removable tilt.
Dimensions: 225×83 in; wb 128 in.

1920
Rolls-Royce (GB)
1920 Pattern, Mk I

Of the many types of wheeled AFVs used by the belligerent powers in World War I the British Rolls-Royce armoured car (Admiralty turreted pattern) was the most numerous. The armoured body was built on the civilian 'Silver Ghost' car chassis. Shortly after the war the 1920 pattern was introduced. It differed from the original mainly in having disc instead of wire spoke wheels, restyled front wings and other detail modifications.
Engine: six-in-line, petrol, 50 bhp, 7.04 litres.
Transmission: four-speed.
Chassis: ladder type; leaf spring suspension (cantilever type at rear); dual rear tyres.
Bodywork: hull of armour plate (9 mm) with rotating turret mounting Vickers machine-gun; crew three.
Dimensions: 16 ft 7 in × 6 ft 3 in; wb 11 ft 11½ in.

1923
Renault (F)
MH 10CV 'Dragon'

After the First World War designers tried various drive configurations for cross-country vehicles, including 4×4, 6×4, half-track and full-track. Seen here is a Renault 6×4 truck of the British Royal Army Service Corps. It proved itself in the Sahara, concurrently with the Citroën/Hinstin-Kégresse half-track. The British had bought the Renault to study it and as a result several British makers designed similar trucks, starting with Karrier in 1924.
Engine: four-in-line, petrol, 13.9 hp, 2.12 litres.
Transmission: three-speed with two-speed auxiliary gearbox (in unit with foremost rear axle).
Chassis: ladder type; leaf spring suspension (inverted on rear bogie); dual tyres all round.
Body: open test body with seating for six plus driver.
Dimensions (chassis): 4.27 × 1.89 m; wb 2.57 + 0.90 m.

1924
Skoda (ČS)
PA2

The Skoda 'PA2' armoured car was produced during 1924–25 and featured four-wheel drive. Steering was on all wheels, but for normal use either the front or rear wheels could be locked in straight-ahead position. The car could be driven in either forward or rearward direction at up to 60 km/h. Armament consisted of four machine-guns and the combat weight was seven tons. Tyre size was 40×8, ground clearance 310 mm.

Engine: four-in-line, petrol, 80 bhp, 9.73 litres.

Transmission: four-speed forward and reverse.

Chassis: ladder type; leaf spring suspension.

Body: armoured hull (8 mm) of symmetrical shape; crew five.

Dimensions: 6.20×2.20 m; wb 3.76 m.

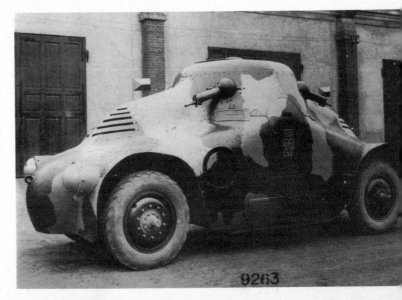

1925
Thornycroft (GB)
'Hathi' Mk II

Shortly after the Great War the British RASC assembled a four-wheel drive tractor, using components taken from captured German Daimler and Erhardt gun towers. The vehicle was named 'Hathi' (Hindustani for elephant). In October 1923 the War Department issued specifications for a purpose-built 4×4 tractor. It was built by Thornycroft in Basingstoke and designated 'Hathi' Mk II. The first was demonstrated in October 1924 and about two dozen were made subsequently. Some saw service in Australia (until WW II) and India. A 6×6 modification was built also.

Engine: six-in-line, petrol, 90 bhp, 11.2 litres.
Transmission: dual-ratio three-speed (6F2R); permanent all-wheel drive.
Chassis: ladder type; leaf spring suspension.
Body: open cab and wooden body with hoops and tilt.
Dimensions: 16 ft 4 in × 6 ft 10½ in; wb 11 ft 6 in.

1926
Fiat/Spa/Pavesi (I)
P4 mod. 26

The Pavesi articulated (twin-unit)
tractor was conceived just before
World War I as a steel-wheeled 4×4
agricultural tractor. Invented by Ing.
Pavesi of Pavesi & Tolotti (who made
heavy 4×2 tractors during World War
I) and in 1924 a modified version was
accepted by the Italian Army as an
artillery tractor. Quantity production
was by the Spa division of Fiat, from
1926. With various modifications it
was made until 1942. Shown are two
tractors working in tandem.
Engine: four-in-line, petrol, 40 bhp,
4.7 litres.
Transmission: four-speed;
permanent all-wheel drive.
Chassis: jointed construction,
articulating in horizontal and vertical
planes, the latter for steering.
Bodywork: open cab on front unit;
cargo/personnel body with tilt on
rear unit.
Dimensions: approx. 3.90×2.08 m;
wb 2.32 m.

1927
Morris-Commercial (GB)
D-Type

The D-Type Morris-Commercial was a 30-cwt 6×4 truck, developed mainly for military purposes but available for civilian use. The military authorities used relatively large numbers of them with a variety of body styles including GS cargo, ambulance, tanker, house-type van, tractor for semi-trailer, etc. Specimen seen here was photographed on its first outing in Singapore in 1927. It carried a mock-up 'armoured car' body with Vickers machine-gun in large turret.

Engine: four-in-line, petrol, 35 bhp, 2.51 litres.

Transmission: four-speed with two-speed auxiliary gearbox.

Chassis: ladder type; leaf spring suspension (twin inverted on rear bogie).

Body: wooden 'armoured car' with turret.

Dimensions (chassis): 15 ft 3¼ in × 5 ft 9½ in; wb 8 ft 6 in + 3 ft 4 in.

1929
Ford/SYS (USA/NL)
AA

Throughout the 1920s endeavours were made to achieve good cross-country performance for trucks at reasonable cost, the latter requirement being logical and unavoidable in peacetime. The Dutch Ford organization asked the Schiedamse Yzer—en Staalbewerking (SYS) N.V. (now NETAM) of Schiedam to convert a Model AA Ford truck chassis. It was done by attaching balancing beams/gear cases to the rear wheel hubs and fitting dual-tyred wheels at the (inside) ends of each. This 6×4 conversion system was later perfected by DAF ('Trado').

Engine: four-in-line, petrol, 40 bhp, 3.29 litres.
Transmission: four-speed.
Chassis: ladder type; leaf spring suspension (transversal at front, inverted cantilever type at rear).
Body: none (test vehicle).
Dimensions: wb (mean) 131½ in.

1932
Berliet (F)
VPR2

This 6×6 chassis was of rather un-
orthodox design. It had steering axles
at the front and rear end and a conventional type rear axle with dual
tyres amidships. This configuration
was used for several Berliet cross-
country vehicles, including a command car and an armoured car. Shown
here is an anti-aircraft gun carriage.
The armament consisted of twin
Hotchkiss 13·2-mm machine-guns.
The vehicle had a kerb weight (fully
equipped) of 3,200 kg and could carry
1,300 kg.
Engine: six-in-line, petrol, 51 bhp,
2.74 litres.
Transmission: four-speed with
two-speed transfer.
Chassis: ladder type; four long cantilever type semi-elliptic leaf springs.
Bodywork: open; platform with
tripod-mounted twin AA machine-
guns, ammunition and equipment
lockers and boxes.
Dimensions: 4.80×1.94 m;
wb 1.82+1.75 m.

1933
Büssing-NAG (D)
G31, Kfz.61

Verstärker-Kraftwagen (amplifier vehicle) bodywork on standard 1½-ton 6×4 truck chassis. Similar chassis were supplied by Krupp, Daimler-Benz and Magirus. Many types of open and closed bodywork were fitted on all these chassis throughout the 1930s. They were later superseded by modernized types such as the *'Einheitsdiesel'* but many remained in service during the war. Bodywork shown was typical of the period and similar types were used for other roles like printing, artillery computing, etc.
Engine: four-in-line, petrol, 65 bhp, 3.92 litres.
Transmission: three-speed with two-speed auxiliary gearbox.
Chassis: ladder type; leaf spring suspension (twin inverted on rear bogie).
Body: wooden van type, integral with cab; six side windows, rear door.
Dimensions: 5.70×2.10 m; wb 2.71+0.95 m.

1933
Henschel (D)
33D1

Used by the German Army and Air Force and produced until 1941 with petrol and diesel engine. The latter, 33G1, was made under licence by Magirus, who installed a Deutz diesel engine. Similar types were produced by Büssing-NAG, Daimler-Benz and Krupp. All had 'double-drive' rear bogie (6×4) and the payload capacity varied from 2½-3 ton off roads and 3-4 tons on roads.
Engine: six-in-line, petrol, 100 bhp, 10.86 litres (33G1: 9.12-litre diesel).
Transmission: five-speed.
Chassis: ladder type; leaf spring suspension (inverted on rear bogie).
Body: soft-top cab; dropside body with hoops and tilt (for general and special purposes).
Dimensions: 7.40×2.50 m; wb 3.75+1.10 m.

1934–35
Hillman (GB)
9.8 HP 'Minx'

Small two-seater scout car based on civilian 'Minx' car chassis (available for the mounting of special bodies for £115). It was officially known as 'Hillman Scout, 4 whld, 2 seat' and was allocated War Dept. registration number M35585. Another (fully) armoured car based on Hillman 'Minx' chassis appeared in 1942. Known as 'Gnat', this had the engine transferred to the rear, but neither car went into volume production. The 'Gnat' had a full-length hull and turret-mounted Bren mg.

Engine: four-in-line, petrol, 27 bhp, 1.18 litres.
Transmission: four-speed.
Chassis: ladder type; leaf spring suspension; oversize tyres (6.00-16 instead of 4.50-18).
Body: partly- and lightly-armoured two-seater.
Dimensions: 11 ft 5 in × 4 ft 11 in; wb 7 ft 8 in.

1934
Magirus (D)
M206/P, Sd.Kfz. 263

Officially known as *Panzerfunkwagen (Pz.Fu.Wg.), Sd.Kfz.263*
this armoured communication vehicle was based on a modified
6×4 truck chassis. Similar chassis were produced by Büssing-
NAG and Daimler-Benz. They differed from the original truck
chassis mainly in having duplicate driving controls at the rear.
Similar armoured hulls were for *Sd.Kfz.231* (heavy armoured
car with 2-cm gun) and *Sd.Kfz.232* (ditto with radio equipment).
Supplied until 1936.
Engine: six-in-line, petrol, 70 bhp, 4.56 litres.
Transmission: four-speed with two-speed auxiliary gearbox.
Chassis: ladder type; leaf spring suspension (inverted on rear
bogie); belly-support rollers amidships.
Body: armoured hull with fixed turret and overhead extendable
aerial.
Dimensions: 5.57×1.82 m; wb 2.50+0.90 m.

1935
Kurogane (J)
95 'Black Medal'

This little Japanese four-wheel drive scout car was designed in
1935. About 4,800 were made. Some were fitted with a small
truck body and a closed cab. It had mechanical brakes on the
rear wheels only. Specimen shown was captured by the
American forces in northern New Guinea during the actions
there in April 1944. The 'Black Medal' weighed 1,000 kg and had
a maximum speed of 70 km/h. A few were later used by the
French forces in Indo-China.
Engine: two-in-vee, air-cooled, petrol, 25 bhp, 1399 cc.
Transmission: three-speed.
Chassis: semi-backbone type with five cross-members; coil
spring independent front suspension, leaf springs at rear.
Body: open 3/4-seater with folding top and side screens.
Dimensions: 3.56×1.50 m; wb 2.00 m.

1935
Phänomen (D)
25H 'Granit', *Kfz.31*

Most widely-used ambulance of the German forces during the 1930s was the Phänomen *'Granit'*. It had carrying capacity for four stretchers or eight sitting cases and the cab was either soft-top, hard-top with open sides (side curtains provided) or enclosed, as shown. A spare wheel was carried on both sides of the rear end of the body. Vehicle shown has survived in Britain, where it came after many years of service with the Spanish Army.

Engine: four-in-line, petrol, air-cooled, 37 bhp, 2.5 litres.
Transmission: four-speed.
Chassis: ladder type; leaf spring suspension.
Body: integral van type with side windows and double rear doors; four stretchers.
Dimensions: 5.40×2.05 m approx.; wb 3.60 m.

1935
Lancia (I)
3 RO N Mil.

This was one of the standardized heavy trucks *(Autocarro Unificato Pesante)* of the Italian Army. Similar-looking trucks were produced by Fiat. They were widely-used throughout World War II. Some had solid rubber tyres. For starting the engine the vehicle had an inertia starter unit forward of the crankshaft; this unit was handcranked. A petrol power unit was used in the Lancia 3 RO B, the 3 RO N (N = *Nafta*, diesel) had a Junkers-type diesel engine. (Photo: IWM NA 1798).

Engine: five-in-line, two-stroke with reciprocating pistons, 93 bhp, 6.87 litres.
Transmission: five-speed with two-speed auxiliary gearbox.
Chassis: ladder type; leaf spring suspension.
Body: hard-top cab with half-doors and side screens; wooden body with hoops and tilt.
Dimensions: 7.08×2.35 m; wb 4.30 m.

47

1936
Morris-Commercial (GB)
PU/Mk 2

During the late 1930s several British firms supplied 8-cwt trucks based on light 4×2 chassis, as well as some on 4×4 chassis. Shown is the 4×2 variant of Morris-Commercial Cars Ltd. All had a similar basic body with a removable waterproof cover and tubular structure enabling the cover to be used off the vehicle as a shelter. Some were used as personnel/cargo carriers, others were fitted with wireless equipment. (Photo: IWM E197).
Engine: six-in-line, petrol, 60 bhp, 3.48 litres.
Transmission: four-speed.
Chassis: ladder type; leaf spring suspension.
Body: open cab with half-doors and canvas top; well type body with three seats, lockers, etc.
Dimensions: 13 ft 10 in × 6 ft 4 in; wb 8 ft 0 in.

1936
GUY (GB)
'Ant'

The Guy 'Ant' was a 15-cwt 4×2 truck which went into production during the mid-1930s. A four-wheel drive variant, the 'Quad-Ant' was introduced later. 15-cwt 4×2 trucks were also supplied by Commer, Ford, Morris-Commercial and Vauxhall (Bedford), all making use of commercial truck components as far as was possible. The 'Ant' had an unusual gear change pattern, opposite to the normal type. Unfamiliar drivers sometimes started in top gear, then produced terrible noises when trying to change up (into a lower gear!).
Engine: four-in-line, petrol (Meadows), 55 bhp, 3.68 litres.
Transmission: four-speed.
Chassis: ladder type; leaf spring suspension.
Body: open cab with canvas top and side curtains; GS body fitted for wire-laying.
Dimensions: 14 ft 0 in × 6 ft 6 in; wb 8 ft 5 in.

1936
Praga (ČS)
AV

The Praga Model AV 6×4 six-passenger command car was in production during 1936–39. Similar vehicles were produced by Skoda and Tatra on 6×4 and 6×6 chassis. The Praga weighed 2,180 kg and had 5.50-18 tyres, single rear. The maximum speed was 92 km/h with fuel capacity of 81 litres providing a range of about 300 km. Two spare wheels were carried on top of the luggage compartment at the rear.

Engine: six-in-line, petrol, 70 bhp, 3.46 litres.
Transmission: three-speed with two-speed transfer.
Chassis: ladder type; independent suspension with torsion bars at front, leaf springs at rear.
Body: four-door six-seater with folding top, half-doors and side screens.
Dimensions: 5.10×1.75 m; wb 2.50+0.92 m.

1937
Auto Union (Horch)   (D)
EFm, *Kfz.15, m.E.Pkw.*

During the late 1930s and early 1940s the German forces acquired quantities of three types of standardized four-wheel drive car chassis — light, medium and heavy — for the mounting of various body types. The medium type shown here was used, mainly with passenger-carrying and van bodywork, the latter for signals roles. Until 1940 this chassis was also produced by Opel. The spare wheels were mounted on stub axles.
Engine: eight-in-vee, petrol, 80 bhp (or Opel six-in-line, 68 bhp).
Transmission: four-speed with two-speed transfer.
Chassis: ladder type; coil spring independent suspension.
Body: open four-seater with four half-doors, folding top and side screens.
Dimensions: 4.74×1.85 m; wb 3.10 m.

1937
Opel   (D)
3.6-36S 'Blitz'

The Opel 'Blitz' three-tonner, which technically had much in common with the American Chevrolet and the British Bedford (all three belonging to the General Motors Corporation), was one of the most widely-used trucks of the German forces during World War II. It proved so satisfactory that in 1944 Daimler-Benz was brought in to co-produce it (instead of their own Mercedes-Benz L3000S truck). There was also a 4×4 version of the 'Blitz', as well as a long-wheelbase bus chassis and lighter versions.
Engine: six-in-line, petrol, 68 bhp, 3.63 litres.
Transmission: five-speed.
Chassis: ladder type; leaf spring suspension.
Body: all-steel two-seater closed cab; dropside wood/steel cargo body with tarpaulin.
Dimensions: 6.10×2.26 m; wb 3.60 m.

50

1937
Fiat/Spa (I)
AS37

'AS37' stood for *'Autocarro Sahariano 1937'* or Sahara truck, Model 1937. It was derived from the standard Italian military truck 'TL37', which was, in turn, a truck version of the *'Trattore Leggero'* (light artillery tractor). Further variants were the 'TL37' Tipo Libia *(Trattore Artigliera Libia* — Libya artillery tractor), the 'TL37' *Carro Libia* (Libya truck) and the TL37 *Carro Pontiere* (bridging truck). They all differed from the 'TL37' standard truck in various details. 'AS37' shown had 11.25-24 tyres ('TL37': 9.00-24 or semi-pneumatic 160×881).

Engine: four-in-line, petrol, 57 bhp, 4.05 litres.

Transmission: five-speeds; individual drive shafts to all wheels.

Chassis: ladder type; coil spring independent suspension.

Body: composite wood and steel cab and body with canvas tilt and side extensions.

Dimensions: 4.70×2.10 m approx.; wb 2.50 m.

1937
Steyr (A)
640

In 1931 the Steyr-Daimler-Puch combine introduced a 6×4 Austro-Daimler 72-bhp-engined truck, designated ADG (from 1936 ADGR). In 1935 it was supplemented by a lighter model, the Steyr 440 with 45-bhp power unit. This 440 was superseded by the 640 (shown) in 1937. Produced for the Austrian Army, the German *Wehrmacht* and its allies until 1941, with 1½-ton cargo and ambulance bodywork.

Engine: six-in-line, petrol, 55 bhp, 2.26 litres.

Transmission: four-speed with two-speed transfer (in unit with middle axle).

Chassis: ladder type; leaf spring suspension (inverted on swing axles of rear bogie); stub axle-mounted spare wheels.

Body: open cab with folding top and side curtains; wooden body with hoops and tilt.

Dimensions: 5.33×1.73 m; wb 2.50+1.06 m.

1937
MAN (D)
HWA526D, *I.E.Lkw*

Standardized six-wheel drive light truck, designed by the German *Heereswaffenamt* and produced during 1937–40 by Daimler-Benz, Henschel, Magirus and MAN. Popularly-known as *'Einheitsdiesel'* it was intended to replace the various 6×4 types produced during the 1930s. It appeared with several body types, including 'house type' vans for signals and similar equipment and had a good cross-country performance. Shown is a MAN-built specimen equipped with snow-chains.

Engine: six-in-line, diesel (Kämper), 85 bhp, 6.23 litres.

Transmission: four-speed with two-speed transfer.

Chassis: ladder type; coil spring independent suspension all round.

Body: standard fixed-side body with hoops and tilt, used for general and special purposes.

Dimensions: 5.85×2.26 m; wb 3.10+1.10 m.

1938
Mercedes-Benz (D)
170V, *Kfz. 11*

The '170V' of Daimler-Benz was one of many civilian type car chassis to be fitted with military *'Kübelsitzer'* bodywork. The body illustrated here was one of several types. Front end and wings were standard, rear wings were cut to increase angle of departure. Front bumpers were always replaced by the narrower and deeper type shown. The windscreen could be folded forward and the doors were easily removable.

Engine: four-in-line; petrol, 38 bhp, 1.7 litres.
Transmission: four-speed.
Chassis: X-pattern; independent suspension with transversal leaf spring at front, coil springs at rear.
Body: four-seater open with folding top, half-doors and side screens.
Dimensions: 4.11 × 1.58 m; wb 2.84 m.

1938
Rába Botond (H)
38M

This 1½-ton 6×4 cross-country truck with stub axle-mounted spare wheels was designed and built by Magyar Vagon-és Gépgyár (Hungarian Railway-Carriage and Machine Works). This firm was founded in 1896 and between 1902 and 1925 licence-produced Praga cars and trucks, followed by Austro-Fiat (from 1925) and Krupp (from 1936) trucks and buses. Between 1940 and 1944 when the works were destroyed by bombing, the firm also produced aircraft. Today Rába produces trucks as well as axles and other components.

Engine: four-in-line; petrol, 65 bhp, 3.77 litres.
Transmission: five-speed.
Chassis: ladder type; leaf springs at front; independent suspension with wishbones and twin coil springs at rear.
Body: open cab with folding top; wooden body with hoops and tilt.
Dimensions: 5.75 × 2.20 m; wb 2.47 + 1.12 m.

1938
FN (B)
63C/4RM

As the model designation suggests, this was the 4RM (*Quatre Roues Motrices* — four-wheel drive) version of the FN Model 63C truck. The 63C had been introduced in 1937 as a 5-ton 4×2 commercial truck; the 63C/4RM *Tracteur-Porteur Tout Terrain* (1938–40) was a derivation intended as an artillery tractor. Apart from the front-wheel drive, modifications included larger wheels and tyres (single rear) and a rotating cylindrical drum at front to prevent 'rooting' in ditches and to facilitate driving through brush, etc.

Engine: six-in-line, petrol, 65 bhp, 3.94 litres.
Transmission: four-speed with two-speed transfer.
Chassis: ladder type; leaf spring suspension.
Body: closed cab; composite wood/steel rear body with hoops and tilt.
Dimensions: 5.68×2.30 m, wb 2.70 m.

1939
Volkswagen (KdF) (D)
Typ 82, *Kfz.1*

The German KdF 'People's Car' (Volkswagen) had hardly been introduced when the military version, known as *'Kübelwagen'* made its appearance and saw service on all fronts. Its air-cooled engine was suitable for hot as well as extremely cold conditions. The *'Kübel'* shown here (captured by the British) has special desert tyres at rear. Today it is a collector's item. (Photo: IWM E30954).
Engine: horizontally-opposed air-cooled four-cylinder, petrol, at rear, 24 bhp, 985 cc (later production: 25 bhp, 1131 cc).
Transmission: four-speed, in unit with limited-slip differential.
Chassis: platform type; torsion bar independent suspension.
Body: open four-seater with four half-doors, folding top and side screens.
Dimensions: 3.74×1.60 m; wb 2.40 m.

1939
Fiat (I)
508C Mil.

The giant Fiat concern produced a wide variety of military vehicles for the Italian armed forces and for export. Among the smallest was this *'Torpedo Militare'* tourer type field car, based on the contemporary 'Balilla' car chassis. It was produced until the end of the war. Seen on the right is an OM *'Autocarretta' Tipo 32* four-wheel steer 4×4 'mountain truck'.
Engine: four-in-line, petrol, 32 bhp, 1.09 litres.
Transmission: four-speed.
Chassis: ladder type; independent front, conventional rear suspension.
Body: open four-seater with four half-doors, folding top and side screens.
Dimensions: 3.61×1.48 m; wb 2.43 m.

1939
Commer (GB)
Q4

Typical British Army 'GS' load carrier (3-ton, 4×2), based on 'Superpoise' commercial truck chassis. Main differences with commercial type were 10.50-16 tyres on WD pattern split wheels, radiator guard and standard 'GS' body. Early models still had the standard tyres (twin rear). Similar trucks were supplied by Austin and Vauxhall (Bedford); these were better liked by RASC drivers because, unlike the Commer, they had servo-assisted brakes.

Engine: six-in-line, petrol, 81 bhp, 4.08 litres.
Transmission: four-speed.
Chassis: ladder type; leaf spring suspension.
Body: all-steel closed cab; standard GS body with flat floor, hoops and canvas tilt.
Dimensions: 21 ft 1 in×7 ft 1$\frac{1}{2}$ in; wb 13 ft 9 in.

1939
AEC (GB)
0853 'Matador'

During 1939–45 AEC produced over 9,000 'Matador' tractors, the majority of which were fitted with bodywork as shown. These bodies provided seating for additional crew members and space to carry stores and equipment and, in the case of the Army's medium artillery tractor, ammunition. Most 'Matadors' operated by the RAF had a platform body with side sills or van body for signals equipment.
Engine: six-in-line, diesel, 95 bhp, 7.58 litres (some had petrol engines).
Transmission: four-speed with two-speed transfer.
Chassis: ladder type; leaf spring suspension.
Body: closed cab with removable top; composite construction body (with steel-panelled roof on early models).
Dimensions: 20 ft 9 in × 7 ft 10½ in; wb 12 ft 7½ in.

1939
Faun (D)
ZR

This heavy Faun *Zugmaschine* (road tractor) was in production during 1939–46. It weighed 10,000 kg and in bottom gear had a drawbar pull of 5,500 kg. Designed for towing full-trailers over good roads. Max. road speed 60 km/h. The tractor shown was used by the German Air Force (*Luftwaffe*). There was also a modified version (ZRS) for use on railroads. The triangle on the cab roof indicated that a trailer was being towed; this was swung forward when operating solo.

Engine: six-in-line, diesel (Deutz), 150 bhp, 13.54 litres.

Transmission: four-speed with overdrive gear set between clutch and gearbox (providing total of 8F2R)

Chassis: ladder type; leaf spring suspension.

Body: large four-door cab, seating seven; ballast body at rear.

Dimensions: 6.45 × 2.44 m; wb 3.60 m.

1939
Scammell (GB)
SV/2S 'Pioneer'

During 1939–46 Scammell Lorries Ltd produced nearly 1,500 of these heavy breakdown tractors. Although the crane was light (3-ton max. lift) and the road speed low (24 mph) the vehicle had tremendous towing and winching capacity. Overall ratio in bottom gear was 111:1. The bogie comprised gear cases, swivelling about the (single) rear axle ends. There was a vertical-spindle winch under the body with 8-ton line pull and 450 ft of $\frac{7}{8}$-in diameter rope.
Engine: six-in-line, diesel (Gardner), 102 bhp, 8.4 litres.
Transmission: six-speed (OD top); final drive by gear train bogie.
Chassis: ladder type; leaf spring suspension.
Body: three-seater cab with half-doors; rear body with sliding jib crane and equipment lockers.
Dimensions: 20 ft 3 in×8 ft 6 in; wb 10 ft 0$\frac{1}{4}$ in+4 ft 3$\frac{1}{4}$ in.

60

1939
White (USA)
M3A1

The White-built Scout Car, M3A1, was standardized in 1939 and consisted of a four-wheel drive truck-type chassis with armoured hull. Much the same vehicle but with the rear axle and wheels replaced by a rubber-tracked bogie (half-track) was later produced by White, Autocar and Diamond T. The scout car, M3A1, was also supplied to allied armies. Photo (IWM: H13861) shows his late Majesty King George VI reviewing armoured division in September 1941.

Engine: six-in-line, petrol (Hercules), 110 bhp, 5.24 litres.
Transmission: four-speed with two-speed transfer.
Chassis: ladder type; leaf spring suspension.
Body: open top armour-plate hull with hoops and tilt; hinged armour shields for windscreen and side windows; crew eight.
Dimensions: $221\frac{1}{2} \times 77$ in; wb 131 in.

1940
Hillman (GB)
10HP Mk II

'Light Utility' body, based on Hillman 'Minx' passenger car chassis. Shown is a Mk II version as used by the RAF. There were several other Marks, all with minor detail differences, as well as all-enclosed van versions. Model shown had two seats in the cab and two folding seats immediately behind (back of cab was open to main body). They were used for a variety of purposes and similar vehicles were supplied by Austin and Morris, based on their respective 10HP car chassis.
Engine: four-in-line, petrol, 30 bhp, 1.18 litres.
Transmission: four-speed.
Chassis: integral construction; leaf spring suspension.
Body: closed cab; rear body with drop tailboard, hoops and tilt with opening sections at forward end.
Dimensions: 12 ft 7 in × 5 ft 3 in; wb 7 ft 8 in.

1940
Chevrolet (IND)
1311X3

American Chevrolet ½-ton 4×2 commercial chassis, produced in Canada (RHD), assembled in India and fitted with Indian military pattern 15-cwt GS (general service) bodywork. Special oversize tyres for use in the deserts of North Africa. Similar bodywork was fitted on Canadian/Indian Ford ½-ton 4×2 chassis. These vehicles were produced during 1939–42 and some of the Chevrolets were used by the famous 'Long Range Desert Group' (together with various other types of Chevrolets). (Photo: IWM E1348).
Engine: six-in-line, petrol, 78 bhp, 3.5 litres.
Transmission: three-speed.
Chassis: ladder type; leaf spring suspension.
Body: open cab with folding top and side curtains; composite wood and metal GS body with hoops and tilt.
Dimensions: wb 113½ in.

1940
Austin (GB)
K2/Y

Most common ambulance of the British armed forces during World War II. It was used by several other countries as well, especially after the war. Over 13,000 were made at Austin's Longbridge works, where production was almost continuous from 1940 until the war ended. In much smaller quantities the same type of body was also fitted on Bedford and Morris-Commercial chassis. Several of the Austins still exist in the hands of vehicle collectors.

Engine: six-in-line, petrol, 60 bhp, 3.46 litres.

Transmission: four-speed.

Chassis: ladder type; leaf spring suspension.

Body: open-sided cab; accommodation in main body for attendant and four stretchers or ten sitting cases; door between cab and body; double doors at rear.

Dimensions: 18 ft 0 in × 7 ft 3 in; wb 11 ft 2 in.

1940
Chevrolet (CDN)
C30

Canadian Military Pattern 30-cwt 4×4 truck, produced by General Motors of Canada Ltd (shown) and Ford Motor Co. of Canada Ltd (with Ford mechanical components). 1941 production had small detail changes to front end, 1942–45 models had completely restyled cab. Truck shown was one of many supplied to Britain at the beginning of the war. There was also a 3-ton version, as well as other body variants.

Engine: six-in-line, petrol, 85 bhp, 3.5 litres.

Transmission: four-speed with two-speed transfer.

Chassis: ladder type; leaf spring suspension.

Body: all-steel cab and GS body with 18-in hinged side panels, tubular superstructure and tilt.

Dimensions: 201×84 in; wb 134 in.

1940
Opel (D)
3,6-6700A 'Blitz'

In appearance the 4×4 version of the Opel *'Blitz'* 3-tonner differed from the basic 4×2 type in having a longer front overhang (wheelbase was shorter) and being somewhat higher. Except for the steering ends the driven front axle was similar to the rear axle. Clearly visible is the Notek blackout light which was fitted on practically all vehicles produced in Germany during the war. (Photo: IWM BU 11193).

Engine: six-in-line, petrol, 73.5 bhp, 3.63 litres.

Transmission: five-speed with two-speed transfer.

Chassis: ladder type; leaf spring suspension.

Body: all-steel cab; tanker body (*T Stoff Wagen*) for V-2 missile equipment.

Dimensions: 6.00×2.20 m approx.; wb 3.45 m.

1940
Fordson (GB)
WOT1

Largest wartime production vehicle of the British Ford Motor Company was the 3-ton 6×4. This chassis was supplied to the RAF and fitted with numerous body types, including the air crew coach shown here (after demob). Similar bodywork was mounted on the Austin K6 6×4 and US Dodge VK62B 4×2 chassis. It provided seating for twenty-three and had light luggage racks along the sides. There was a speaking-tube to the driver's cab.

Engine: eight-in-vee, petrol, 85 bhp, 3.62 litres.
Transmission: four-speed (some with auxiliary gearbox).
Chassis: ladder type; leaf spring suspension (inverted on rear bogie).
Body: closed cab, seating two; composite construction main body with metal outer panels and double rear doors.
Dimensions: 24 ft 0 in × 7 ft 4 in; wb 11 ft $1\frac{1}{4}$ in + 3 ft $6\frac{1}{4}$ in.

1940
Ford (CDN)
FGT

Gun tractor variant of range of
Canadian Military Pattern vehicles,
produced by Ford (shown) and General Motors in Canada for Canadian,
British and other Commonwealth
nations. Equipped with four-wheel
drive and power winch. After 1945
these vehicles were in service with
other armies for many more years.
The bodywork of the gun tractor was
very similar to the British pattern as
mounted on Morris-Commercial C8
and Guy 'Quad Ant' chassis.
Engine: eight-in-vee, petrol, 95 bhp,
3.9 litres.
Transmission: four-speed with
two-speed transfer.
Chassis: ladder type; leaf spring
suspension.
Body: all-enclosed steel body with
two side doors and accommodation
for six men (driver, mate and crew of
four).
Dimensions: 170×88 in;
wb 101¼ in.

1941
Moto Guzzi (I)
'Trialce'

One of a range of motortricycles produced by Moto Guzzi for the Italian Army. This *'Trialce porta mitraglia'* carried three men and a machine-gun. The machine-gun could be fitted either on the pedestal mount as shown or on a tripod which was carried on the back of the vehicle. There were also other body versions. Carrying capacity varied from 350–500 kg. Tyre size was 3.50-19, max. speed just over 70 km/h.
Engine: single-cylinder, horizontal, petrol, 13.2 bhp, 0.5 litre.
Transmission: four-speed with auxiliary gearbox.
Chassis: tubular construction; girder type front fork.
Body: open two-seater rear body with locker and spare wheel.
Dimensions: 2.82×1.24 m; wb 1.88 m.

1941
Humber (GB)
'Snipe'

During the early years of the war the Rootes Group supplied several variants of their Humber (Super) Snipe including saloons, heavy utility cars and 8-cwt trucks. Illustrated is the tourer model with bodywork by Thrupp & Maberly. This became well known because Field Marshal Montgomery used one ('Old Faithful') in the North African Campaigns and another during 1944/45 on the Western fronts. Shown here, General Alexander and Lord Louis Mountbatten, during the Victory Parade in London, 1946.
Engine: six-in-line, petrol, 85 bhp, 4.08 litres.
Transmission: four-speed.
Chassis: ladder type; independent front suspension with transversal leaf spring, conventional at rear.
Body: four-door five-seater with folding top and side screens.
Dimensions: 15 ft 0 in×5 ft 10 in; wb 9 ft 6 in.

1941
Ford (CDN)
C11AD

Basically this was a 1941 American Ford station wagon, produced in Canada (RHD) for use by Field Marshal Alexander. Main variations from the standard model were that a full-floating truck type rear axle and special wheels with 9.00-13 tyres were fitted. The bodywork was extensively 'militarized' and featured a 'soft top'. In order to retain sufficient stiffness after removing the top, the doors were made an integral part of the body structure.

Engine: eight-in-vee, petrol, 95 bhp, 3.9 litres.
Transmission: three-speed.
Chassis: ladder type; transversal leaf spring at front, conventional leaf springs at rear.
Body: open four/five-seater with folding top; no doors.
Dimensions: 194×79 in; wb 114¼ in.

1941
Steyr (A)
1500A

Throughout World War II Austria produced vehicles of various types for the German armed forces. One was the Steyr 1500A which was a four-wheel drive light truck chassis. It appeared with a variety of body types, including personnel (shown), command, van and truck. When it proved to be a very good vehicle the German Auto Union was brought in to boost its production. Daimler-Benz and Phänomen supplied similar vehicles on their own chassis.

Engine: eight-in-vee, petrol, air-cooled, 85 bhp, 3.52 litres.
Transmission: four-speed with two-speed transfer.
Chassis: ladder type; independent front, conventional rear suspension.
Body: open eight-seater with four half-doors, folding top and side screens.
Dimensions: 5.08×2.00 m; wb 3.25 m.

1941
Dodge (USA)
T116-WD21

At the beginning of World War II the British used a wide variety of ambulances, many of which were donated by private individuals and civilian organizations. The vehicle shown is basically a commercial Dodge 1-ton panel delivery van, fitted out as an ambulance, operated by the RASC for the British Volunteer Ambulance Corps and carried the usual military markings as well as the name of the donor.

Engine: six-in-line, petrol, 85 bhp, 3.56 litres.
Transmission: three-speed.
Chassis: ladder type; leaf spring suspension.
Bodywork: all-steel integral type van; accommodation for driver, attendant, two stretchers and four sitting cases.
Dimensions: $223\frac{1}{2} \times 67\frac{1}{2}$ in; wb 133 in.

1941
Bedford (GB)
MWC

Widely-used 15-cwt 4×2 chassis, fitted with 200-gallon water tank with engine-driven pump (earlier production had two manual pumps). At the front of the chassis was a pump which was driven by the engine starter dog and used to pick up water from any available source. Water passed through filters and chlorinators for purification. Similar equipment on Morris-Commercial 'CS8' 15-cwt 4×2 chassis. Bedford MW chassis was also used with 'GS' cargo and other body types.
Engine: six-in-line, petrol, 72 bhp, 3.5 litres.
Transmission: four-speed.
Chassis: ladder type; leaf spring suspension.
Body: soft-top cab with half-doors (open type on early models); 200-gallon water tank and pumping equipment.
Dimensions: 15 ft 3½ in × 6 ft 6½ in; wb 8 ft 3 in.

1941
Bedford (GB)
QLC

One of 52,245 3-ton 4×4 Bedford trucks produced by Vauxhall Motors during World War II. There were several body types including 'GS' cargo, troop carrier, Bofors gun tractor, signals van, etc. Truck shown was fitted with aircraft fueller body at a later date. The equipment comprised an 850-gallon fuel tank (AVGAS) with a 100-gallon lubricating oil compartment at the forward end, two fuel pumps at rear (driven by separate engine), three 13-ft elevating booms, each with 12-ft hose and trigger type nozzle, etc.

Engine: six-in-line, petrol, 72 bhp, 3.5 litres.
Transmission: four-speed with two-speed transfer.
Chassis: ladder type; leaf spring suspension.
Body: closed cab (removable top half); AVGAS fueller equipment with booms.
Dimensions: 19 ft 7 in×7 ft 3 in; wb 11 ft 11 in.

1941
Studebaker (USA)
US6-U2

The Studebaker Corp. produced almost 200,000 2½-ton six-wheelers (6×4 and 6×6), similar in general design to those made by GMC (q.v.) and International. The 'Studes', however, were produced mainly for Lend-Lease (international aid) whereas the 'Inters' were for the USMC and USN. Russia received more than half of all the Studebakers produced, others went to Britain, like the short-wheel-base cargo truck with Heil winch shown here. There were several other variants.
Engine: six-in-line, petrol (Hercules), 87 bhp, 5.34 litres.
Transmission: five-speed (OD top) with two-speed transfer.
Chassis: ladder type; leaf spring suspension (inverted on rear bogie).
Body: closed cab (open type used also), steel cargo body with troop seats and tilt.
Dimensions: 244×88 in; wb 126+44 in.

1941
Büssing-NAG (D)
4500A

Widely-used 4½-ton 4×4 cargo truck of German *Wehrmacht*, produced during 1941–45. There was also a 4×2 (rear-wheel drive only) version, designated '4500S' and both appeared with various types of open and closed bodywork. Their immediate predecessors, which differed only in detail, were the '500A' and '500S' of 1940–41. After 1945 they were continued in production for some time as Büssing '5000A' and '5000S' with increased carrying capacity (5.4 tons).
Engine: six-in-line, diesel, 105 bhp, 7.41 litres.
Transmission: five speed (OD top) with single-speed transfer.
Chassis: ladder type; leaf spring suspension.
Body: three-seater cab; dropside cargo body with hoops and tilt.
Dimensions: 8.16×2.35 m; wb 4.80 m.

1941
Mack (USA)
NO

Prime mover for heavy artillery such as the 8-in howitzer and 155-mm gun, this 7½-ton 6×6 vehicle became later known as the 'Super Mack'. A special gun coupling attachment was provided together with a crane to raise and lower the gun trails to and from the coupling. Vehicle shown was operated by the Belgian Army long after the war and has a non-original cab. A 40,000-lb capacity winch was fitted under the front bumper.

Engine: six-in-line, petrol, 159 bhp, 11.58 litres.
Transmission: five-speed with two-speed transfer.
Chassis: ladder type; leaf spring suspension (inverted on rear bogie).
Body: coachbuilt cab (originally soft-top type); wooden body with hoops and tilt. Also with steel body.
Dimensions: 297×103 in; wb 127+58 in.

1941
Daimler (GB)
Armoured Car

Main producers of armoured cars in Great Britain during World War II were Daimler and the Rootes Group. Daimler produced two Marks (I and II) of its 'Armoured Car, Daimler'. It had four-wheel drive with separate drive shafts to each wheel and disc brakes and generally was a more sophisticated vehicle than the Humber. It could be driven both forward or rearward, having duplicate driving controls at the rear.

Engine: six-in-line, petrol, at rear, 95 bhp, 4.09 litres.
Transmission: five-speed forward and reverse (pre-selective type).
Chassis: unitary construction; double coil spring independent suspension.
Body: hull of 16-mm armour plate; turret-mounted 2-pounder gun with co-axial Besa machine-gun.
Dimensions: 13 ft 0 in × 8 ft 0 in; wb 8 ft 6 in.

1941
Fiat/Spa (I)
AB41 'Autoblindata'

The 'AB40' was armed with three 8-mm machine-guns (two in turret), the 'AB41' had a turret-mounted 20-mm gun and two mgs, the 'AB43' (final model) had a 47-mm gun and two mgs. The 'AB41' and 'AB43' weighed about 7½ tons. They had duplicate driving controls at rear so that the car could be driven in either direction.

Engine: six-in-line, petrol, at rear, 100 bhp (AB40: 80, AB43: 110 bhp), 4.99 litres.
Transmission: six forward and reverse gears; individual propeller shafts to each wheel (X layout).
Chassis: self-supporting hull; independent coil spring suspension all round.
Body: all-steel riveted hull; crew four; spare wheels on sides (on stub axles).
Dimensions: 5.09 × 1.93 m; wb 3.25 m.

1941
Büssing-NAG (D)
GS, *Sd.Kfz.233*

Heavy armoured car with short 7.5 cm gun (*Schwerer Panzerspähwagen 7.5 cm*) on all-wheel steer 8×8 standard chassis produced by Büssing-NAG. This chassis was known as *'8 Rad Einheitswagen'* and was fitted with various types of hull (*Sd.Kfz. 231, 233, 263*). The *Sd.Kfz. 233* was used as a close-support vehicle. An improved model had a Tatra air-cooled V-12-cylinder diesel engine and air brakes. Designated *Sd.Kfz. 234* it was produced with various armaments.

Engine: eight-in-vee, petrol, rear-mounted, 180 bhp, 7.91 litres.
Transmission: three-speed with two-speed and reverse transfer, providing total of 6F6R.
Chassis: ladder type; independent suspension all round with inverted semi-elliptic leaf springs.
Body: armour plate hull (5–15 mm); crew four.
Dimensions: 5.85×2.20 m; wb 1.35+1.40+1.35 m.

1942
Willys (USA)
MB 'Jeep'

Probably the best-known (and most-imitated) military vehicle of all time was the 'Truck, $\frac{1}{4}$-ton, 4×4, Command Reconnaissance'. It was produced by Willys-Overland and co-produced by the Ford Motor Co. It was used by all Allied forces (as well as the enemy) and after the war, during which nearly 640,000 were made, it saw service in many other countries. Vehicle shown is treated to a well-deserved wash in a stream in Luxembourg, September 1944.

Engine: four-in-line, petrol, 54 bhp, 2.2 litres.
Transmission: three-speed with two-speed transfer.
Chassis: ladder type; leaf spring suspension.
Bodywork: all-steel 2+2-seater with folding canvas top.
Dimensions: $132\frac{1}{4}$×62 in, wb 80 in.

1942
Volkswagen (KdF) (D)
Typ 166, *Kfz.1/20*

Designed by Porsche, this *'Schwimmwagen'* (amphibious car) was produced in considerable quantities by the *Volkswagenwerke* during 1942–44. It differed from the *'Kübelwagen'* (q.v.) mainly in having a watertight hull, four-wheel drive, an extra low ratio in the transmission, and a hinged propeller at the rear. The propeller could be swung down to engage (via a chain-drive and sprocket clutch) with the engine crankshaft, providing a speed in water of about 10 km/h.
Engine: horizontally-opposed air-cooled four-cylinder, petrol, at rear, 25 bhp, 1.13 litres.
Transmission: five-speed.
Chassis: unitary construction; torsion bar independent suspension.
Body: all-steel open-top hull with folding top; no doors.
Dimensions: 3.82×1.48 m; wb 2.00 m.

1942
Dodge (USA)
T214-WC52 'Beep'

Most common of the standardized range of US $\frac{3}{4}$-ton 4×4 vehicles was the Weapons Carrier, popularly known as 'Beep'. Shown is a winch-equipped model. There were many other body types including command and radio cars, ambulances, etc. A 6×6 (six-wheel drive) version was also produced. All were supplied by the Chrysler Corporation. The Canadian Chrysler plant produced the 'Beep' with slightly different engine.
Engine: six-in-line, petrol, 92 bhp, 3.77 litres.
Transmission: four-speed with single-speed transfer (two-speed on 6×6 version).
Chassis: ladder type; leaf spring suspension.
Bodywork: open two-seater cab; steel body with tilt and troop seats.
Dimensions: $176\frac{1}{2}×82\frac{3}{4}$ in; wb 98 in.

1942
Chevrolet (USA)
NJ-G-7107

The Chevrolet Division of General
Motors was the main supplier of
1½-ton 4×4 trucks for the US and
Allied forces. With the main excep-
tions of engine, transmission and rear
axle it was very similar to the GMC
2½-ton 6×6. Picture shows a convoy
of new trucks leaving the Fort Wayne
Quartermaster Depot in January
1942. In addition to the cargo version
shown, these chassis were supplied
with many other body types.
Engine: six-in-line, petrol, 93 bhp,
3.8 litres.
Transmission: four-speed with
two-speed transfer.
Chassis: ladder type; leaf spring
suspension.
Body: closed cab, seating two; steel
cargo body with troop seats and
canvas tilt.
Dimensions: 224×86 in; wb 145 in.

81

1942
GMC (USA)
CCKW-353

The famous GMC 'deuce-and-a-half' (2½-ton, 6×6) was the work-horse of the US Army during World War II. In common with other standardized chassis, there was a large number of body types and equipment variations. Shown is a cargo truck with open cab and winch. Others had a closed cab and/or no winch. GMC built over half a million of these trucks and after the war they remained popular all over the world for many years for military and civilian use.

Engine: six-in-line, petrol, 104 bhp, 4.4 litres.
Transmission: five-speed (OD top) with two-speed transfer.
Chassis: ladder type; leaf spring suspension (inverted on rear bogie).
Body: open cab with canvas top and side screens; wooden cargo body (steel type used also) with troop seats and tilt.
Dimensions: 270×88 in; wb 142+44 in.

1942
GMC (USA)
DUKW-353 'Duck'

This amphibious truck was first designed in 1941/42 and subsequently built in large numbers by General Motors, based on their well-proven 2½-ton 6×6 truck chassis. It was very successful in many landing operations, carrying troops and supplies from ships to shore. The tyre pressure could be regulated from the driver's seat to obtain maximum grip on beach sand, roads and other surfaces. The 'Duck' remained operational in many countries until the 1970s.
Engine: six-in-line, petrol, 104 bhp, 4.4 litres.
Transmission: five-speed (OD top) with two-speed transfer and water propeller drive.
Chassis: integral construction; leaf spring suspension (inverted on rear bogie).
Body: steel hull; open driver's compartment with folding top; cargo compartment with hoops and tilt; accommodation for twenty-five men.
Dimensions: 372×99 in; wb 142+44 in.

1942
Leyland (GB)
WLW3A 'Retriever'

British producers of 3-ton 6 × 4 chassis were AEC, Albion, Austin, Crossley, Ford, Guy, Karrier, Leyland and Thornycroft. All were supplied with several body types, including GS cargo, bridging, searchlight, etc. Illustrated is a workshop body (No. 4 Mk III) on the Leyland chassis. The centre parts of the body sides hinged to fold to horizontal position for extra floor space, or to double-fold position for working on from ground level. Earlier 'Retrievers' did not have the fixed windscreen shown here.

Engine: four-in-line, petrol, 73 bhp, 5.9 litres.

Transmission: four-speed with two-speed auxiliary gearbox.

Chassis: ladder type; leaf spring suspension (inverted on rear bogie).

Body: open cab with canvas top and side curtains; flat-floor main body with hoops and tilt; fitted 7.5 kW generator.

Dimensions: 22 ft 5½ in×7 ft 5¼ in; wb 11 ft 0 in+4 ft 0 in.

1942
Autocar (USA)
U-7144T

Standardized 4–5-ton 4×4 chassis, used exclusively as tractor truck (fitted with 'fifth-wheel' semi-trailer coupling on rear of chassis). Main producers were Autocar and White. Similar but not identical tractors were built by Federal. Autocar also produced a somewhat larger variant (5–6-ton Model U-8144T). Both closed (shown) and open cabs were fitted. Semi-trailers were of various open (cargo) and closed types.
Engine: six-in-line, petrol (Hercules), 112 bhp, 8.6 litres.
Transmission: five-speed (OD top) with two-speed transfer.
Chassis: ladder type; leaf spring suspension.
Body: all-steel two-seater cab (soft-top type supplied also); tread plate platform across frame behind cab.
Dimensions: 203×95 in; wb 134½ in.

1942
FWD (USA)
SU-COE

Militarized cab-over-engine (COE) version of commercial model 'SU' truck, supplied mainly to Britain for use as medium artillery tractor. Four-wheel drive was permanent, i.e. front drive could not be disengaged as on most 4×4 vehicles. There was, however, a (lockable) third differential in the transfer case so that maximum traction was obtained at all times without 'wind up' in the drive line. Bodywork was similar to that of the AEC 'Matador' artillery prime mover. (Photo: IWM H 11484).
Engine: six-in-line, petrol (Waukesha), 126 bhp, 7.57 litres.
Transmission: five-speed with chain-drive single-speed transfer.
Chassis: ladder type, leaf spring suspension.
Body: closed cab with two seats; composite wood/steel body with seating for ten, side doors and tilt.
Dimensions: 265×93½ in; wb 144 in.

1942
Škoda (ČS)
175 'Radschlepper Ost'

Designed by Porsche this huge machine was produced in small
quantity by the Škoda concern in Czechoslovakia during 1942
for the German Army. It was intended for artillery towing on the
very poor roads of the Eastern front in Russia, hence the large
(1.50 m diameter) all-metal wheels, all of which were driven.
Later they were used in France and the Low Countries also.
Latil in France produced a similar tractor for the *Wehrmacht*,
for the same purpose.
Engine: four-in-line, air-cooled, petrol (some diesel), 90 bhp,
6.02 litres (separate petrol engine for starting, 12 bhp, 565 cc).
Transmission: five-speed.
Chassis: ladder type; leaf spring suspension.
Body: large closed cab; dropside body with hoops and tilt.
Dimensions: 5.47×2.30 m; wb 3.00 m.

1942
Tatra (ČS)
T111

During the German occupation of Czechoslovakia, the Czech
industry was engaged in producing equipment, including trucks
and AFVs, for the *Wehrmacht*. Most vehicles thus produced were
pre-war designs but the heavy 'T111' 6×6 truck was newly
introduced in 1942. The German designation was Tatra 6500/
111, 6500 indicating the payload in kgs. An $8\frac{1}{2}$-tonner (8000/
111) was also made. Technically these Ledwinka-designed
vehicles were very sophisticated and cross-country performance
was of a high order.
Engine: twelve-in-vee, air-cooled, diesel, 175 or 210 bhp,
14.82 litres.
Transmission: four-speed with two-speed auxiliary gearbox.
Chassis: tubular backbone; independent suspension with
swing axles and leaf springs (quarter-elliptic at front).
Body: closed cab; dropside body with hoops and tilt.
Dimensions: 8.55×2.50 m; wb 4.17+1.122 m.

1942
White (USA)
1064

The 10-ton White cargo truck shared its front end with the 6-ton model '666' but did not have front-wheel drive. It was used for long-distance haulage of supplies, particularly in the Middle East. Mack built a very similar truck, using its own mechanical components, front end and cab (many of the Macks had a soft-top cab). On top of the White cab was a carrying platform with 7-in sides. Tyres were 11.00-24 at front, 14.00-20 at rear. A spare was carried for both sizes.

Engine: six-in-line, diesel (Cummins), 150 bhp, 11 litres.

Transmission: five-speed (OD top).

Chassis: ladder type; leaf spring suspension (inverted on rear bogie).

Body: closed cab, seating three; wooden cargo body with folding troop seats, hoops and tilt (also with steel body).

Dimensions: 327×97 in; wb 174+52 in.

1942
Thornycroft (GB)
WF/AC6/2 'Amazon'

During the war Thornycroft produced 1,820 'Amazon' chassis for electrically-operated, turntable-mounted Coles cranes. The generator which provided the power to operate the hoisting, derricking and slewing motors was driven from the truck's gearbox PTO (power take-off). Earlier 'Amazons' (1939–42 Model WF/AC6/1) had a civilian type radiator grille, later production (1944–45 Model WF8/NR6) had longer wheelbase and a diesel engine. They were used by the RAF for various hoisting operations. Max. lift 5 tons at 7-ft radius.

Engine: six-in-line, petrol, 100 bhp, 7.76 litres.
Transmission: four-speed with two-speed auxiliary gearbox.
Chassis: ladder type; leaf spring front suspension, rigid beam rear bogie suspension.
Body: closed cab; Coles EMA petrol-electric crane, powered by PTO-driven 250-volt DC generator.
Dimensions: 30 ft 0 in × 7 ft 9 in; wb 9 ft 6 in + 4 ft 6 in.

1942
Humber (GB)
Scout Car, Mk I, II

Of the almost 11,000 scout cars produced in Great Britain during World War II just over 6,600 were produced by Daimler ('Dingo'), the remainder by the Rootes Group under the official designation 'Car, Scout, Humber', Mk I and Mk II. Both Marks were basically similar. Many of their mechanical components were the same as used for other Humber 4×4 military vehicles but the engine was mounted at the rear. Armament consisted of a Bren machine-gun.
Engine: six-in-line, petrol, at rear, 87 bhp, 4.1 litres.
Transmission: four-speed with two-speed transfer.
Chassis: ladder type; independent front suspension with transversal leaf spring, conventional rear suspension.
Body: open-top hull of 14-mm armour plate; crew two or three.
Dimensions: 12 ft 7 in × 6 ft 2½ in; wb 7 ft 7 in.

1943
GAZ (USSR)
GAZ-67B

During World War II the Red Army received large quantities of US military vehicles and other equipment under the Lend-Lease agreement. Included were many thousands of 'Jeeps'. In 1942 the Soviets designed their own field car, designated 'GAZ-64', later 'GAZ-67'. In 1943 it went into quantity production, with minor modifications, as 'GAZ-67B' and as such it was made until 1953. Many saw service in the Korean war. The engine was much like the old American Ford model 'A'.
Engine: four-in-line, petrol, 54 bhp, 3280 cc.
Transmission: four-speed with single-speed transfer.
Chassis: ladder type; leaf spring suspension (quarter-elliptic at front).
Body: open four-seater with folding top.
Dimensions: 3.35 × 1.69 m; wb 2.10 m.

1943
Toyota (J)
SUKI

Amphibious truck with four-wheel drive and two-ton payload carrying capacity. A total of just under 200 of these amphibians were made during 1943. The mechanical components were inherited from the limited-production Toyota model 'KC' medium 4×4 truck. Toyota trucks at that time had many details in common with the American Chevrolet which during the 1930s was produced in Japan.

Engine: six-in-line, petrol, 63 bhp, 3.39 litres.

Transmission: four-speed with two-speed transfer and water propeller drive.

Chassis: integral construction; leaf spring suspension.

Body: welded steel hull, decked forward of the enclosed driver's compartment.

Dimensions: 7.62×2.22 m; wb 4.00 m.

1943
Diamond T (USA)
969B

Typical application of standardized US Army 4-ton 6×6 truck: the famous wrecker. The Diamond T Car Co. of Chicago was the almost-exclusive supplier of 4-ton 6×6 chassis and they were fitted with a variety of bodies, including cargo, dump and van. The wrecker had Holmes W-45 twin-boom equipment (over 10,000 of which were supplied, mainly for this chassis type). Wrecker shown operated on the 'Red Ball Express' supply route in W. Europe.

Engine: six-in-line, petrol (Hercules), 119 bhp, 8.6 litres.

Transmission: five-speed (OD top) with two-speed transfer.

Chassis: ladder type; leaf springs (inverted on rear bogie).

Body: open cab with canvas top and half-doors; steel rear body with two swivel booms and power winches; telescopic brace legs at either side. Also with closed cab.

Dimensions: 292×100 in; wb 125+52 in.

1943
Corbitt (USA)
50SD6

Designed for the US Coast Artillery the 6-ton 6×6 cargo and prime mover truck was used also for other towing and load carrying. The standardized chassis was produced also by White, Brockway and others, from 1941. Mack built a similar truck but with different front end and cab. A25,000-lb capacity winch was located between cab and body. Other body types existed also. Early models had a closed cab.

Engine: six-in-line, petrol (Hercules), 180 bhp, 14 litres (early models 12.76 litres, 165 bhp).
Transmission: four-speed with two-speed transfer.
Chassis: ladder type; leaf spring suspension (inverted on rear bogie).
Body: soft-top cab; standard wooden (or steel) body with troop seats, hoops and tilt.
Dimensions: 289×96 in; wb 159+52 in.

1943
Pacific (USA)
TR-1/M26

Known as the 'Dragon Wagon' this armoured tractor truck (12-ton, 6×6, M26, produced by Pacific Car & Foundry Co. of Seattle, Wash.) and tank-transporter semi-trailer (40-ton, 8-wheel, M15, produced by Fruehauf) was designated as 40-ton Tank Transporter Truck-Trailer, M25. In 1944 the semi-trailer was modified to take a 45-ton payload and the armoured cab was replaced by a 'soft-skin' type.

Engine: six-in-line, petrol (Hall Scott), 230 bhp, 17.86 litres.
Transmission: four-speed with three-speed transfer; Knuckey rear bogie with chain drive.
Chassis: ladder type; leaf spring suspension at front, balancing beams at rear.
Body: armoured cab for crew of seven, including driver.
Dimensions: tractor: 304×131 in; wb $140\frac{1}{2}$+63 in.
semi-trailer length: 465 in.

1943
Ford (USA)
GAK-M20

High-mobility armoured command, personnel and cargo vehicle, based on the 'M8' armoured car (which carried a rotating turret with 37-mm gun). The 'M20', officially known as 'Armored Utility Car', was fitted with a ring mount for a .50 calibre machine-gun. Both the 'M8' and the 'M20' could travel at 55 mph and had a cruising range of about 350 miles. The 'M8' armoured car was known by the British as 'Greyhound' and was noted for its quietness of operation.
Engine: six-in-line, petrol (Hercules), at rear, 110 bhp, 5.24 litres.
Transmission: four-speed with two-speed transfer.
Chassis: integral construction; leaf spring suspension (inverted on rear bogie).
Body: armour-plate hull, open-topped; crew two to six, depending on role.
Dimensions: 197×100 in; wb 80+48 in.

1944
Chevrolet (CDN)
C8A

Smallest in the range of Canadian Military Pattern vehicles was the Heavy Utility, a box-shaped all-steel body on a short 4×4 chassis. They were used, with suitable modifications, for various roles, principally personnel carrier (HUP), Wireless (HUW) and ambulance (HUA). Shown is a late model, restored by the editor in the early 1960s. Earlier models (1942–43) had 'run-flat' combat tyres and did not carry a spare; instead they had an extra side door.

Engine: six-in-line, petrol, 85 bhp, 3.5 litres.

Transmission: four-speed with single-speed transfer.

Chassis: ladder type; leaf spring suspension.

Body: semi-forward control; three side doors, one rear door; sliding roof at rear.

Dimensions: 163×79 in; wb 101 in.

1944
Austin (GB)
K6/A

The Austin 3-ton 6×4 range first
appeared in 1939, the 'Breakdown
Gantry' in early 1944. Until then,
similar bodywork had been fitted on
forward-control 3-ton 6×4 chassis
produced by Crossley, Guy, Leyland,
etc. The body superstructure sup-
ported a longitudinal runway with
hand-operated travelling block. The
forward end of the (sliding) runway
could be dropped to the floor for
higher lift at the rear. $10\frac{1}{2}$ cwt of
ballast was fitted at the front of the
chassis.

Engine: six-in-line, petrol, 83 bhp,
3.99 litres.
Transmission: four-speed with
two-speed transfer.
Chassis: ladder type; leaf spring
suspension (inverted on rear bogie).
Body: closed cab, seating two;
composite body, partly flat, partly
well type; gantry type crane with
max. lift of $2\frac{1}{2}$ tons.
Dimensions: 20 ft 3 in×7 ft 6 in;
wb 10 ft 9 in+4 ft 0 in.

1944
Leyland (GB)
'Hippo' Mk II

The Leyland 'Hippo Mk II' Series was introduced in 1944 and over 1,000 were produced, mainly for long-distance haulage of supplies on the mainland of Europe following D-day. The bodies (GS cargo) were made by Edwards Brothers (Tippers) Ltd. After the war many were fitted with specialist van type bodies. The 'Mk IIA' model had dual tyres on the rear wheels, the 'Mk IIB' had singles again, like the 'Mk II' shown. The 'Mk I' was of pre-war design with open cab.

Engine: six-in-line, diesel, 100 bhp, 7.4 litres.
Transmission: five-speed with two-speed auxiliary gearbox.
Chassis: ladder type; leaf spring suspension (inverted on rear bogie).
Body: closed cab with removable top; composite construction GS main body with hoops and tilt.
Dimensions: 27 ft 3 in × 8 ft 1 in; wb 13 ft 2½ in + 4 ft 7 in.

1944
Ward LaFrance (USA)
1000 Series 5/M1A1

This heavy wrecker with swinging boom crane and comprehensive recovery equipment was standardized as 'M1A1' in 1944 and was produced by Ward LaFrance and Kenworth to the same specification. It replaced a variety of types made by the same firms and which were, until then, standardized as 'M1'. The 'M1A1' had winches at front and rear and carried welding and cutting equipment, jacks, tow chains, towbar and other items. After the war it was used by NATO and other armies as well as civilian operators for many years.

Engine: six-in-line, petrol (Continental), 133 bhp, 8.2 litres.
Transmission: five-speed (OD top), with two-speed transfer.
Chassis: ladder type; leaf spring suspension (inverted on rear bogie).
Body: open cab with canvas top and side screens; heavy crane with telescopic support legs; equipment lockers, etc.
Dimensions: 281 (without crane jib) × 100 in; wb 155 + 52 in.

1944
Ford (CDN)
C29SR 'Lynx'

Officially known as 'Car, Scout, Ford II, Lynx II' this machine was the Canadian equivalent of the British BSA/Daimler 'Dingo' scout car. Unlike the 'Dingo', which had a frame-less hull with independent suspension, the 'Lynx' had a conventional chassis frame and rigid truck type axles. The hulls were produced by the International Harvester Co. in Canada. Vehicle shown was slightly modified and has spare wheel, replacing equipment locker at front end. Crew: two (driver and observer). Speed 57 mph.

Engine: eight-in-vee, petrol, at rear, 95 bhp, 3.9 litres.
Transmission: four-speed with two-speed transfer.
Chassis: ladder type; leaf spring suspension.
Body: open-top hull, made of homogeneous armour plate of welded construction; escape hatch on each side; canvas top.
Dimensions: 144×73 in; wb 82 in.

1945
Albion (GB)
FT15N

Light field artillery tractor with six-wheel-drive. This high-mobility vehicle was developed during 1944/45 but only about 150 were produced before the requirement ceased, due to the end of the war. The vehicle was designed to provide a very low silhouette. It could be made even lower by removing the cab and body superstructure. A Turner 8-ton worm-drive winch was fitted and the complete vehicle weighed just under 6 tons.

Engine: six-in-line, petrol, 95 bhp, 4.56 litres.
Transmission: four-speed with two-speed transfer.
Chassis: ladder type; leaf spring suspension (twin inverted on rear bogie).
Body: two-seater cab with removable top and side screens; crew compartment seating six, behind cab; steel rear body with hoops and tilt.
Dimensions: 20 ft 11 in×7 ft 7½ in; wb (mean) 12 ft 6 in.

H 5884088

1946
GAZ (USSR)
GAZ-63A

Although the truck illustrated was produced later, the 'GAZ-63A' 1½-ton 4×4 made its first appearance just after the war. It was similar in layout to the wartime US Chevrolet 1½-ton 4×4, many of which were supplied to the Soviet Union under Lend-Lease. There were several variants, including the 'GAZ-63' (similar but without the winch), the 'GAZ-63D' tractor truck, etc., as well as 4×2 versions, the cargo truck of which was designated 'GAZ-51'. They were produced at the Gor'kiy Automobile Plant.
Engine: six-in-line, petrol, 70 bhp, 3.48 litres.
Transmission: four-speed with two-speed transfer.
Chassis: ladder type; leaf spring suspension.
Body: closed steel cab; wooden cargo/personnel body with hoops and tilt.
Dimensions: 5.80×2.20 m; wb 3.30 m.

1948
Ford/M.-H. (USA/B)
F6

At the end of World War II there were ample supplies of surplus military vehicles for all armies to build up sufficient inventories. These vehicles, after overhaul, served for many years. Among the relatively few new vehicles of that period which did have military characteristics like four-wheel drive was the American Ford COE chassis with Marmon-Herrington front-wheel drive, used by the Belgian Army for artillery towing. Assembled by the Antwerp Ford plant, this chassis was fitted with other body types also.
Engine: six-in-line, petrol, 95 bhp, 3.62 litres.
Transmission: four-speed with two-speed transfer.
Chassis: ladder type; leaf spring suspension.
Body: std front end; coach-built body with accommodation for crew, equipment and ammunition (later models had sloping rear roof panel).
Dimensions: 5.75×2.25 m; wb 3.40 m.

1950
Delahaye (F)
VLR

Most vehicle-producing countries produced at least pilot models of vehicles comparable with the ubiquitous wartime US 'Jeep', hoping to get orders from their respective governments. Some manufacturers succeeded, others had to rely mainly on commercial customers who were not always forthcoming. The 'Jeep' reigned supreme and even replaced this Delahaye after only a few years of production for the French Army (the Hotchkiss-built 'Jeep' was almost identical to the wartime Willys 'MB' and was produced in France until 1969).

Engine: four-in-line, petrol, 63 bhp, 1.99 litres.
Transmission: four-speed with two-speed transfer.
Chassis: ladder type; independent suspension with torsion bars and trailing arms.
Body: four-seater with folding top and side screens.
Dimensions: 3.46×1.57 m; wb 2.15 m.

1950
Dodge (USA)
T245/M37

To replace the 1942–45 Dodge ¾-ton 4×4 T214 'Beep' range the US forces during the 1950s and 1960s acquired over 80,000 of these modernized post-war models. Shown is the Truck, ¾-ton, 4×4, Cargo w/Winch, 'M37', fitted with arctic equipment. There were other body options but far fewer than on the wartime chassis. Exterior variations consisted of a canvas cab top, spare wheel mounting on left-hand side of cab and omission of winch. First saw active service in Korea.
Engine: six-in-line, petrol, 94 bhp, 3.77 litres.
Transmission: four-speed with two-speed transfer.
Chassis: ladder type; leaf spring suspension.
Body: closed cab (removable hard top); steel body with hoops and tilt.
Dimensions: 189×73½ in; wb 112 in.

1950
Reo (USA)
M34

Post-war replacement for the ubiquitous GMC 2½-ton 6×6 was the Reo 'Eager Beaver', as it was known originally. Later it was produced also by Studebaker, Kaiser Jeep, and others. Shown is the 'M34' which had single rear tyres. The 'M35' was similar but had dual rear tyres and a flat-floor cargo body. Both were available with front-mounted winch. The basic chassis was used for numerous other body styles and in later years a diesel or multi-fuel engine was installed in certain models.
Engine: six-in-line, petrol, 146 bhp, 5.42 litres.
Transmission: five-speed with two-speed transfer.
Chassis: ladder type; leaf spring suspension (inverted on rear bogie).
Body: soft-top cab; steel body with troop seats, hoops and tilt.
Dimensions: 262×88 in; wb 130+48 in.

1950
Diamond T (USA)
M52

The 5-ton 6×6 'M-series' replaced the various wartime 4-, 6- and 7½-ton models. Models to the same specification were produced by International, Kaiser Jeep (now AM General Corp.) and Mack. The 'M52' tractor truck version illustrated was later available with a Mack diesel engine ('M52A1'). For the military assistance programme (MAP) a Cummins diesel-engined variant was made, designated 'M818'. Optional fitments were a front-mounted winch and a hard top.
Engine: six-in-line, petrol (Continental), 196 bhp, 9.86 litres.
Transmission: five-speed with two-speed transfer.
Chassis: ladder type; leaf spring suspension (inverted on rear bogie).
Body: soft-top cab; fifth wheel coupling for semi-trailer (shown: Semi-Trailer, Stake, 12-ton, 4-wh., M127).
Dimensions (tractor): 273×97 in; wb 140+54 in.

1950
Leyland (GB)
'Martian'

The Leyland 'Martian' was available for military and civilian use, the military version being designated 'FV1100' Series. There were several variants; shown is the 'FV1103' 'Tractor, 10-ton, 6×6, C.T. Medium Artillery'. The chassis was equipped with an engine-driven 10-ton winch with 350-ft rope. Two-line air brakes were fitted, as well as a controller for electrically-actuated trailer brakes. (Photo: British Official).
Engine: eight-in-line, petrol (RR), 215 bhp, 6.52 litres.
Transmission: four-speed with three-speed transfer.
Chassis: ladder type; leaf spring suspension (transversal at front, with 'walking beams' at rear).
Body: extended cab for crew of 12; rear body for 4½ tons of ammunition and stores.
Dimensions: 26 ft 10¼ in ×8 ft 6 in; wb 12 ft 2½ in +4 ft 7 in.

1950
Scammell (GB)
'Explorer'

Designated FV11301 this British Army 'Tractor, 10-ton, 6×6, G.S. (Scammell), Recovery' was developed from the wartime Scammell 6×4 Heavy Breakdown. Its main role was the recovery of wheeled vehicles and armoured cars. It had a main winch rated at 15 tons and a power-operated jib winch. The average maximum road speed when travelling solo was about 30 mph and the cruising range about 315 miles. It was commercially available.

Engine: six-in-line, petrol, 181 bhp, 10.35 litres.
Transmission: six-speed.
Chassis: ladder type; leaf spring suspension (transversal at front, with 'walking beams' at rear).
Body: three-seater cab; crane at rear with various lockers for tools and equipment.
Dimensions: 20 ft 7½ in × 8 ft 6 in; wb 9 ft 4½ in + 4 ft 3¼ in.

1951
GMC (USA/CDN)
M220CDN

In 1950/51 the GMC Truck & Coach Division of General Motors started producing a new 'Jimmy Deuce-and-a-Half', concurrently with the Reo 'Eager Beaver'. Both 2½-ton 6×6 trucks saw active service in Korea. The GMC was subsequently produced in Canada also and illustrated is a shop van truck made in Canada in 1955. Other variants were cargo, dump, tanker and tractor trucks. All had 'Hydramatic' transmission, some had a front-mounted winch.

Engine: six-in-line, petrol, 130 bhp, 4.94 litres.
Transmission: dual-range automatic with single-speed transfer.
Chassis: ladder type; leaf spring suspension (twin inverted on rear bogie).
Body: hard-top cab; shop van type rear body for signals equipment.
Dimensions: 266 × 96 in; wb 132 + 48 in.

1951
Panhard (F)
EBR

French high-speed armoured car with very good cross-country performance. Originally conceived in 1940 this rather complicated vehicle normally ran on the four rubber-tyred front and rear wheels (4×4). For off-road use the centre wheels could be lowered and driven (8×8). There were duplicate driving controls at rear and the turret mounted a 75-mm gun (in 1967 replaced by a 90-mm gun). (Photo: E. C. Armées).
Engine: horizontally-opposed air-cooled twelve-cylinder, petrol, 200 bhp, 6 litres.
Transmission: two four-speed gearboxes.
Chassis: unitary construction; coil spring independent suspension.
Body: armour-plate symmetrical hull, crew four.
Dimensions: 5.56×2.43 m; wb 4.67 m.

1952
Fiat (I)
639N2/CM52

The Fiat '639N2' 4-ton 4×4 medium truck was standardized by the Italian Army in 1952 as 'CM52' (*Autocarro Medio 1952*). It was later redesignated model '6601'. It was basically a commercial design, equipped with four-wheel drive and some relatively minor modifications in order to meet military requirements (cab roof hatch, military lighting equipment, etc.). The Fiat '639N/CM50', its predecessor, had a petrol engine. Other trucks in this category were supplied by Alfa Romeo, Autobianchi and Lancia.
Engine: six-in-line, diesel, 92 bhp, 6.65 litres.
Transmission: four-speed with two-speed transfer.
Chassis: ladder type; leaf spring suspension.
Body: closed cab, seating two; steel cargo body with fixed sides, removable hoops and tilt.
Dimensions: 6.19×2.37 m; wb 3.27 m.

1952
AEC (GB)
0860 'Militant' Mk 1

The 'Militant' was the most common
10-ton 6×6 truck in the British Army
for many years. Shown is the
'FV11002' artillery tractor version
which was but one of a range of
variants. In this role it towed medium
and heavy Anti-Aircraft guns and
related equipment. The 'Militant'
chassis was also produced without
front-wheel drive (6×4 Model '0859')
and both were available for export.
They were superseded by the Mk 3
'Militant' in 1966.
Engine: six-in-line, diesel, 150 bhp,
11.30 litres.
Transmission: five-speed with
two-speed transfer.
Chassis: ladder type; leaf spring
suspension (inverted on rear bogie).
Body: closed cab; rear body for crew
of 7 with kit and 4½ tons of
ammunition and/or cargo.
Dimensions: 24 ft 2 in×8 ft 0 in;
wb 10 ft 7½ in+4 ft 6 in.

1953
Willys (USA)
MDA/M170

The 'M170' front line ambulance was based on a long-wheelbase version of the 'M38A1' $\frac{1}{4}$-ton 4×4 utility truck. These two vehicles were militarized versions of the Jeep 'Universal' models 'CJ6' and 'CJ5' respectively. In 1963 Willys became Kaiser Jeep and the marque name for all vehicles built by the company became 'JEEP'. In 1970 the company became a subsidiary of the American Motors Corp. and the name was changed to Jeep Corporation. The 'M170' carried three stretchers or six sitting cases (or two and three respectively).
Engine: four-in-line, petrol, 72 bhp, 2.2 litres.
Transmission: three-speed with two-speed transfer.
Chassis: ladder type; leaf spring suspension.
Body: open with folding top, removable canvas doors and side screens.
Dimensions: 155×60$\frac{1}{2}$ in; wb 101 in.

1953
Tatra (ČS)
T805

The 'T805' 1$\frac{1}{2}$-ton 4×4 truck was designed by Tatra but volume production took place in several other nationalized Czech vehicle manufacturing plants also. It was the standard truck in its class and was also exported and available for civilian purposes. In addition to the cargo body seen here several other types were fitted, including 'house type' van. The cab was virtually identical to that of the Praga 'V3S' (q.v.).
Engine: eight-in-vee, petrol, air-cooled, 75 bhp, 2.54 litres.
Transmission: four-speed with two-speed transfer.
Chassis: tubular backbone type; swing axles with hub reduction gears and torsion bars.
Body: closed steel cab; wooden dropside cargo body with hoops and tilt.
Dimensions: 4.72×2.29 m; wb 2.70 m.

1953
DAF (NL)
YA-328

High-mobility 3-ton 6×6 cargo truck and artillery prime mover of the Netherlands Army. It was first introduced in 1950 as 2½-ton 6×6 model 'YA-318'. The 'YA-328' was an improved version and was also produced with other body types including fire fighter, office van, mobile workshop, etc. The second pair of wheels were the spare wheels but they were fitted on hubs and provided extra protection against 'bellying'.

Engine: six-in-line, petrol, 131 bhp, 5.55 litres.

Transmission: five-speed (OD top) with two-speed transfer; propeller shafts on both sides, between chassis and wheels ('H-drive').

Chassis: ladder type; independent torsion bar suspension at front, leaf springs with balancing beam type bogie at rear.

Body: soft-top cab with removable doors; steel body with hoops and tilt.

Dimensions: 6.19×2.40 m; wb 2.75+1.30 m.

1953
Praga (ČS)
V3S

This 3-ton 6×6 truck was designed by the old-established firm of Praga but most vehicles were produced in the works of the Avia aircraft firm. Apart from its Tatra-designed air-cooled diesel engine and the 'elevated' (portal-type) axles the 'V3S' was not unlike the various American 6×6 trucks in the 2½- to 5-ton load class. It was also exported, for military and civilian use. Various body types were fitted, including 'house type' van, wrecker and tanker.

Engine: six-in-line, diesel, air-cooled, 95 (later 110) bhp, 7.41 litres.
Transmission: four-speed with two-speed transfer.
Chassis: ladder type; leaf spring suspension (inverted on rear bogie).
Body: closed steel cab; wooden dropside cargo body with hoops and tilt.
Dimensions: 6.91×2.32 m; wb 3.58+1.12 m.

1953
Mack (USA)
M125

One of the largest post-war US Army cargo and prime mover trucks was the 10-ton 6×6 'M125'. In general appearance it looked like a scaled-up 2½-ton 6×6 'M35' or 5-ton 6×6 'M54' but it weighed almost as much as the 'M35' and 'M54' together. It appeared more often as a tractor truck ('M123'), which was frequently used in conjunction with a 'Dragon Wagon' semi-trailer for tank transporting. The 'M125' was used mainly as a tractor for the 8-in howitzer and 155-mm gun and it had a front-mounted winch with 22½-ton line pull. Later production was by Condec.

Engine: eight-in-vee, petrol (LeRoi), 286 bhp, 13.82 litres.
Transmission: five-speed with two-speed transfer.
Chassis: ladder type; leaf spring suspension (inverted on rear bogie).
Body: soft-top cab; steel body with hoops and tilt.
Dimensions: 280×114 in; wb 151½+60 in.

1954
Bedford (GB)
RL

Standard 3-ton 4×4 of the British services during the 1950s and 1960s. It was a modification of a 7-ton 4×2 commercial truck and went into series production in 1952. Shortly afterwards the headlights were moved from the original (higher) position to that shown here. Later still the radiator grille was modified and eventually the payload rating went up to 4 ton. There were many body styles and other variations such as dual rear tyres and shorter wheelbase. There was also an armoured open-top cab.

Engine: six-in-line, petrol 110 (later 130) bhp, 4.93 litres.
Transmission: four-speed with two-speed transfer.
Chassis: ladder type; leaf spring suspension.
Body: steel closed cab; steel body with removable sides and tailboard, hoops and tilt.
Dimensions: 20 ft 10 in × 7 ft 9 in; wb 13 ft 0 in.

1955
Auto Union (DKW)   (D)
F91/4 'Munga'

Prototypes for a $\frac{1}{4}$-ton 4×4 utility
vehicle or field car for the new German
Federal Army were produced in 1954/
55 by Auto Union, Goliath and
Porsche. For some reason or other
the Auto Union 'Munga' (*Mehrzweck
Universal Geländewagen mit All-
radantrieb*) was selected for quantity
production and some 55,000 were
made during 1955–68 for the German
forces as well as some foreign governments and for civilian customers. Six-
and eight-seater versions were also
available.
Engine: three-in-line 897-cc
two-stroke, 40 bhp (later 980 cc,
44 bhp).
Transmission: four-speed with high
and low range (8F2R).
Chassis: ladder type; independent
suspension with transversal leaf
springs.
Body: four-seater with folding top
and four canvas doors.
Dimensions: 3.45×1.70 m;
wb 2.00 m.

1955
Mercedes-Benz (D)
Unimog S404.114

The 'S'-type 'Unimog' 1½-ton 4×4 was developed by Daimler-Benz from the successful Unimog multi-purpose tractor/power plant. The original 'Unimog' appeared in the late 1940s. During the 1950s several variations on the basic theme were introduced and the list of optional equipment (accessories, implements, body types, etc.) grew in order to suit practically every requirement. The 'S' was a long-wheelbase truck variant with an engine more suited for truck rather than low-speed tractor work. Its mobility is phenomenal.

Engine: six-in-line, petrol, 80 bhp, 2.2 litres.

Transmission: six-speed with two reverse.

Chassis: ladder type; coil spring suspension.

Body: soft-top cab; steel dropside body with hoops and tilt.

Dimensions: 4.93×2.15 m; wb 2.90 m.

1956
Fiat/OM (I)
6600/CP56

The OM division of the Fiat concern produced this very American-looking bridging truck (*Autocarro da Ponte*) for the Italian Army and other NATO forces. It was, in fact, patterned largely on the US Army 5-ton 6×6 'M-Series' chassis, 'M139', with stake-body (Truck, Stake: bridge transporting, 5-ton). Mechanical components (engine, transmission, axles, wheels, etc.) were of Italian design. The truck had 14.00-20 tyres and was classed as a 10-tonner. It was produced until 1964.
Engine: six-in-line, petrol, 196 bhp, 10.68 litres.
Transmission: dual-range four-speed with two-speed transfer.
Chassis: ladder type; leaf spring suspension (inverted on rear bogie).
Body: soft-top cab; special steel body for transport of Engineers' bridging equipment.
Dimensions: 9.55×2.92 m; wb 4.75+1.42 m.

1956
Magirus-Deutz (D)
250AE-L 'Uranus'

Heavy six-wheel drive tractor for tank transporter trailers.
Basically a commercial design, it was supplied to several
countries with modifications to meet the military requirements of
the purchasing Government. The tractor shown was used by the
Swiss Army in conjunction with a 16-ton low-loader trailer for
transporting the G13 *Panzerjäger* and other medium-weight
AFVs (for heavier AFVs the Swiss used British Rotinoff Atlantic
and Super Atlantic tractors with 50-ton low-loader).
Engine: twelve-in-vee, diesel, air-cooled (Deutz), 250 bhp,
15.97 litres.
Transmission: six-speed (OD top) with two-speed transfer.
Chassis: ladder type; leaf spring suspension (inverted on rear
bogie).
Body: four-door steel cab; equipment and ballast body with
hoops and tilt.
Dimensions: 7.69×2.50 m; wb 3.75+1.38 m.

1957
Mercedes-Benz (D)
LG315

The Daimler-Benz-built 5-ton 4×4 trucks for the German
Bundeswehr were developed from the 'LG6600', a 'pseudo-
military' 4×4 truck which appeared in 1953. Early production
'LG315s' had a closed cab (like the 'LG6600' and other com-
mercial normal control Mercedes-Benz trucks) but most vehicles
had the German military pattern soft-top type with 'cut-away'
half doors and removable side screens. The radiator grille
remained of the characteristic civilian pattern.
Engine: six-in-line, multi-fuel, 145 bhp, 8.25 litres.
Transmission: six-speed with two-speed transfer.
Chassis: ladder type; leaf spring suspension.
Body: soft-top cab; steel body with hoops and tilt.
Dimensions: 8.12×2.50 m; wb 4.60 m.

1957
ISUZU (J)
TW340

In June 1957 the Isuzu Motor Co. delivered 3,678 2½-ton 6×6 cargo and special purpose trucks to the US administration in Japan. This was done under the Japan-America Military Assistance Vehicle Exchange Program (US Army Procurement Agency, Japan). The trucks were patterned on the US military 'deuce-and-a-half' standard type but were diesel-powered. Isuzu had produced similar trucks (with open cab) from 1953 and basically the same 6×6 model is still available (Model 'TWD').
Engine: six-in-line, diesel, 120 bhp, 6.13 litres.
Transmission: four-speed with two-speed transfer.
Chassis: ladder type; leaf spring suspension (inverted on rear bogie).
Body: soft-top cab; steel body with hoops and tilt.
Dimensions: 7.35×2.35 m; wb 3.42+1.16 m.

1958
MAN (D)
415 L1AR

One of a range of tactical trucks produced by the Maschinenfabrik Augsburg-Nürnberg AG in Munich. The '415L1AR' was one of the smallest and had a 4-ton payload rating. Other 4×4 MANs included the 630 and 640 series, the former being one of the standard truck chassis of the German *Bundeswehr* (Federal Army). The '415' was also produced, under licence, by the Indian Government, for the Indian Army (named Shaktiman and featuring dual rear tyres and some other modifications).
Engine: six-in-line, multi-fuel, 100 bhp, 5.88 litres.
Transmission: five-speed with two-speed transfer.
Chassis: ladder type; leaf spring suspension.
Body: soft-top cab; steel dropside body with hoops and tilt.
Dimensions: length 7.16 m; wb 4.20 m.

1958
ZIL (USSR)
ZIL-157

During World War II the Soviet Union received over 100,000 2½-ton 6×4 and 6×6 trucks from the US under Lend-Lease and a Soviet-made version appeared about 1947. Designated 'ZIL-151' it was produced until 1958 when the improved 'ZIL-157' superseded it. Both types came in several variants (cargo, tractor, tanker, crane, fire fighting, APC, etc.) and were also supplied for export. Equipped with winch and central tyre pressure regulating system (the 'ZIL-151' did not have this latter feature).

Engine: six-in-line, petrol, 109 bhp, 5.55 litres.

Transmission: five-speed (OD top) with two-speed transfer.

Chassis: ladder type; leaf spring suspension (inverted on rear bogie).

Body: closed steel cab; wooden cargo/personnel body with hoops and tilt.

Dimensions: 6.96×2.35 m; wb 3.66+1.12 m.

1958
Alvis (GB)
'Saladin'

This armoured car, designated 'FV601', was developed for use with infantry and armoured formations for reconnaissance and pursuit operations. It had a turret-mounted 76-mm quick-firing gun and two .30 calibre machine-guns and the vehicle could be waded to a depth of 3 ft 6 in without preparation. Another well-known vehicle on the same, albeit front-engined, chassis was the 'Saracen' armoured personnel carrier.

Engine: eight-in-line, petrol (RR), rear-mounted, 160 bhp, 5.66 litres.
Transmission: pre-selective five-speed forward and reverse.
Chassis: integral construction; independent suspension with torsion bars.
Body: armoured hull with rotating turret; crew of three.
Dimensions: 16 ft 1 in (17 ft 3½ in with gun) ×8 ft 3 in; wb 5 ft 0 in + 5 ft 0 in.

1959
FN (B)
AS24

Airportable tricycle (*Tricar Parachutable*), designed by the late Nicholas Straussler in the mid-1950s and produced in quantity, under Straussler licence, by the Belgian Fabrique Nationale d'Armes de Guerre SA (FN). It could carry four soldiers abreast or driver plus 250 kg. For airdrops it could be collapsed into a small (1.04×1.64 m) pack and after landing it would take the crew only about one minute to prepare the vehicle and drive off. Tyres were wide low-pressure 'Lypsoid' type.
Engine: two-stroke 243.5-cc twin, air-cooled, at rear, 15 bhp.
Transmission: four-speed (no reverse).
Chassis: made of steel tubes with lockable sliding side members; springing obviated by special low-pressure tyres.
Body: none; canvas seat for driver plus three men.
Dimensions: 1.84×1.64 m; wb 1.27 m.

1959
Steyr-Puch (A)
700 AP 'Haflinger'

The 'Haflinger' was named after a breed of powerful mountain horse and has been in production (with detail improvements and modifications) since 1959. Basically it is a small four-wheel drive platform carrier, used for conveyance of personnel, cargo, weapons, etc. Its specification is rather sophisticated, including such features as a tubular backbone frame with swing axles, differential locks front and rear, etc. Several other body types exist, including fire fighter.
Engine: horizontally-opposed 643-cc twin, air-cooled, at rear, 24 bhp (later 27 bhp).
Transmission: four-speed (later five-speed).
Chassis: tubular backbone; coil spring independent suspension.
Body: steel platform with two seats in cab, two collapsible seats at rear; hoops with canvas tilt and doors.
Dimensions: 2.83×1.35 m; wb 1.50 m.

1959
Berliet (F)
TBU15CLD

Originally designed by Rochet
Schneider, a company absorbed by
Automobiles M. Berliet during the
early 1950s, the TBU (and GBU)
range of 6-ton 6×6 tactical trucks
went into volume production about
1960. The GBU models were load-
carriers, the TBU were tractors and
wreckers. 'CLD' in the model designation indicates *Camion Lourd de
Dépannage* (heavy recovery truck).
The crane jib could slew through 270°
and lift 10 tons maximum. Two
winches were fitted (7-ton at front,
14-ton at rear).
Engine: six-in-line, multi-fuel,
200 bhp, 14.75 litres.
Transmission: five-speed with
two-speed transfer.
Chassis: ladder type; leaf spring
suspension (inverted on rear bogie).
Body: soft-top cab for crew of four;
hydraulic crane.
Dimensions: 8.88×2.50 m;
wb 3.48+1.45 m.

1959
Thornycroft (GB)
'Mighty Antar' Mk 3

The 'Mighty Antar' first appeared in the early 1950s, as a civilian heavy duty prime mover. It was subsequently supplied to the British and other armies as a tractor for tank transporter duties in conjunction with full- or semi-trailers. One of the latter, in its 'Mk 3' guise, is shown, carrying a 'Centurion' tank and dwarfing an Austin 'Champ' $\frac{1}{4}$-ton 4×4. The 'Mk 3' could also be used as a 'drawbar tractor' after installing a temporary ballast body on the rear.

Engine: eight-in-line, diesel (RR), 333 bhp, 16.20 litres.
Transmission: four-speed with three-speed transfer.
Chassis: ladder type; leaf spring suspension (inverted on rear bogie).
Body: closed cab, crew body and fifth-wheel coupling for 50-ton semi-trailer.
Dimensions (tractor):
28 ft 6$\frac{1}{2}$ in × 10 ft 6 in; wb 13 ft 5 in +5 ft 2 in.

1960
AMC (USA)
M422 'Mighty Mite'

Originally designed by Mr Ben F. Gregory and developed by Mid-America Research Corp. (with Porsche engine) the 'Mighty Mite' was put into series production by the American Motors Corporation in 1960 for the US Marine Corps. 1,250 were built and the first is illustrated here (carrying George Romney, then AMC president, and USMC Brig. Gen. Frederick Leek). Its official designation was: Truck, Utility, $\frac{1}{4}$-ton, 4×4, Lightweight, 'M422'. The 'M422' was succeeded by the somewhat longer 'M422A1' of which 2,672 were produced, until 1963.

Engine: four-in-vee, air-cooled, petrol, 55 bhp, 1.76 litres.
Transmission: four-speed with single-speed transfer.
Chassis: ladder type; independent suspension with quarter-elliptic leaf springs.
Body: aluminium body with two front seats, two fold-down rear seats.
Dimensions: 107×60$\frac{1}{2}$ in; wb 65 in.

1960
Ford (USA)
M151

During the 1950s the Ford Motor Co. developed a new $\frac{1}{4}$-ton 4×4 utility truck which after lengthy trials went into series production in 1960. It was dubbed 'Mutt' (for military utility tactical truck) but GIs incorrectly called it 'Jeep'. The independent rear suspension system had inherent and dangerous oversteer characteristics and after many accidents had occurred this was redesigned. There were several body options, including front line ambulance ('M718') and the 1972 model, 'M151A2', is made by American Motors.
Engine: four-in-line, petrol, 71 bhp, 2.32 litres.
Transmission: four-speed with single-speed transfer.
Chassis: unitary construction; coil spring independent suspension.
Body: open four-seater with folding top, canvas doors and side screens.
Dimensions: 132×64 in; wb 85 in.

1960
Robur (DDR)
LO 1800 AKF

Militarized four-wheel drive derivation from civilian 4×2 truck produced by VEB Robur-Werke in Zittau, East Germany. It was the standard 1$\frac{1}{2}$-ton 4×4 chassis of the East German armed forces during the 1960s and also appeared with 'house type' van bodies (workshop, command post, ambulance). Tyres were 10.00-20 (single rear), maximum speed 80 km/h and payload capacity 2,500 kg on roads, 1,800 kg cross-country.
Engine: four-in-line, petrol, 70 bhp, 3.34 litres.
Transmission: five-speed with two-speed transfer.
Chassis: ladder type; leaf spring suspension.
Body: steel cab with four seats; wooden body with troop seats (12), hoops and tilt.
Dimensions: 5.35×2.36 m; wb 3.02 m.

1960
Faun (D)
L908/54 VA

Heavy Faun 10-ton 6×6 forward control cargo truck of the German *Bundeswehr*. Unlike some other types built by Faun this model had a single front axle and a tandem axle bogie at rear. Some were fitted with a one-ton hydraulic loading crane, situated between cab and main body. The body floor measured no less than 6.70×2.35 m (22×7½ ft). The convoy is led by a pair of Maico 'M250/B' motorcycles (standardized machine of German Army and Border Police, produced 1961–66).

Engine: eight-in-vee, multi-fuel, air-cooled (Deutz), 178 bhp, 12.67 litres.
Transmission: six-speed with two-speed transfer.
Chassis: ladder type; leaf spring suspension (inverted on rear bogie).
Body: soft-top cab; steel body with triple dropsides, hoops and tilt.
Dimensions: 9.65×2.50 m; wb 4.70+1.40 m.

1961
Land-Rover (GB)
Series IIA '88' (Rover 8)

The first production 'Land-Rover' was introduced in 1948 and it was not long before the British armed forces (followed by many others, all over the world) purchased them for military use. Since the Korean War, where it first saw active service, the military 'Land-Rover' was improved in many ways, concurrently with the basic civilian model. Military versions, however, always differed. In 1958 came the Series II, followed by the Series IIA (Rover 8 to the military) in 1961 and III in 1971.

Engine: four-in-line, petrol, 77 bhp, 2.29 litres.
Transmission: four-speed with two-speed transfer.
Chassis: ladder type; leaf spring suspension.
Body: soft-top aluminium bodywork; shown with communications equipment and machine-gun.
Dimensions: 12 ft 5 in×5 ft 6½ in; wb 7 ft 4 in.

1961
Berliet (F)
GBC8KT

Widely-used French 4-ton 6×6
tactical truck, available with a variety
of body styles including cargo, tractor,
wrecker, tanker, tipper, compressor,
etc. Developed from civilian 'Gazelle'
truck but with functional military
pattern front end and cab. 5–7-ton
winch optional. Cargo version shown
is used as troop or load carrier or
artillery tractor (105-mm howitzer).
Also available with 150-bhp diesel
engine and with single rear axle
(4×4). The latter is in service with the
Portuguese Army.
Engine: five-in-line, multi-fuel,
125 bhp, 7.9 litres.
Transmission: six-speed (OD top)
with two-speed transfer.
Chassis: ladder type; leaf spring
suspension (inverted on rear bogie).
Body: soft-top cab; steel body with
bench-type seats, removable sides,
hoops and tilt.
Dimensions: 7.28×2.40 m;
wb 3.31+1.28 m.

126

1961
LeTourneau-Westinghouse (USA)
LARC-V

Developed by the Ingersoll Kalamazoo Division of Borg-Warner Corporation during the late 1950s the 'LARC-V' was produced in quantity during the 1960s by LeTourneau-Westinghouse and Consolidated (Condec). It was officially known as 'Lighter, Amphibious, Resupply, Cargo, 5-ton, 4×4' (hence: 'LARC-V') and was intended to replace the wartime GMC 'DUKW' landing vehicle. One was powered by a 225-hp gas turbine. They were also supplied to other nations, including Australia (shown) and Germany.

Engine: eight-in-vee, diesel (Cummins), rear-mounted, 300 bhp (early models: 270-bhp Ford V8, petrol).

Transmission: automatic; four-wheel drive.

Chassis: integral construction; 'solid' suspension (vehicle relies on its tyres for springing); four-wheel steering.

Body: aluminium hull with driver's cabin at front.

Dimensions: 420×120 in; wb 192 in.

1962
Simca-Marmon (F)
MH600BS

Standardized French Army 1½-ton 4×4 cargo and personnel truck, developed from a French Marmon-Herrington design but produced in quantity from 1964 by Simca (Unic division). Marmon-Herrington SAF later became Marmon-Bocquet and the 'MH600BS' was then officially referred to as SUMB (Simca-Unic-Marmon-Bocquet). It is rather unusual as it is powered by the old but proven side-valve V8 engine which in France was continued in production when Simca took over the French Ford factory.
Engine: eight-in-vee, petrol, 100 bhp, 4.18 litres.
Transmission: four-speed with two-speed transfer.
Chassis: ladder type; coil spring suspension.
Body: soft-top cab; steel body with hoops and tilt.
Dimensions: 5.10×2.10 m; wb 2.90 m.

1963
Henschel (D)
HS3-160A

During World War II all-wheel drive military trucks were made in large numbers and afterwards all-wheel drive became a matter of course for off-road work. Consequently, many truck manufacturers offered civilian 4×4 and 6×6 chassis for use on construction sites and similar duties. Many were also supplied for military service since price-wise they compared very favourably with specially designed tactical trucks. This Henschel 6×6 is a good example.
Engine: six-in-line, diesel, 180 bhp, 11.04 litres.
Transmission: six-speed with two-speed transfer.
Chassis: ladder type; leaf spring suspension (inverted on rear bogie).
Body: steel closed cab; hyd.-operated tipping/sliding platform for loading, transporting and unloading disabled vehicles.
Dimensions (chassis/cab): 9.02×2.50 m; wb 4.54+1.31 m.

1964
Citroën (F)
FOM

This special airportable truck was produced mainly for the French forces overseas (FOM = *Forces d'Outre-Mer*). There were two basic versions: 3-ton 4×4 with 12.00-20 tyres, single rear (shown) and 5-ton 4×4 with 11.00-20 tyres, dual rear. Several body types were fitted such as cargo (shown), shop van, tanker, etc. They were also supplied to several African states including the Cameroons, Chad, Ivory Coast, Mauritania, Senegal and Upper Volta.

Engine: six-in-line, petrol, 140 bhp, 5.2 litres.
Transmission: five-speed with two-speed transfer.
Chassis: ladder type; leaf spring suspension.
Body: soft-top cab; steel cargo/personnel body.
Dimensions: 7.01×2.48 m; wb 4.60 m.

1964
Magirus-Deutz (D)
M178D15A

Originally introduced as the commercial 'Uranus 170A' in 1957 (with Deutz air-cooled V-8 diesel engine) this truck was adopted by the German *Bundeswehr* in militarized form as 'Jupiter' 7-ton 6×6 in 1962. In 1971 a more powerful engine was installed (model 'M180D15A', 180 bhp). Alternative body styles included tipper, wrecker, elevating platform, tractor, etc. Most military versions had a soft-top cab as illustrated.

Engine: eight-in-vee, multi-fuel, air-cooled (Deutz), 178 bhp, 12.67 litres.

Transmission: six-speed with two-speed transfer.

Chassis: ladder type; leaf spring suspension (inverted on rear bogie).

Body: soft-top cab; steel dropside body with hoops and tilt.

Dimensions: 8.05×2.50 m; wb 4.16+1.28 m.

1964
Faun (D)
Z912/21-203

Most of the heavy 6×6 trucks used by the German *Bundeswehr* were supplied by Faun-Werke Nürnberg (Karl Schmidt) at Lauf near Nuremberg. Faun produced many different 6×6 types (as well as 4×4, 8×8 and other configurations) some had two steering front axles, as shown, rather than a tandem rear bogie. This eliminates rear wheel scrub as well as improving control on slippery surfaces. Shown is a gun tractor with 10-ton winch (1964 and 1969).

Engine: twelve-in-vee, air-cooled, multi-fuel (Deutz), 265 bhp, 15.97 litres.
Transmission: six-speed with two-speed transfer.
Chassis: ladder type, leaf spring suspension.
Body: soft-top, forward control cab; dropside body with hoops and tilt.
Dimensions: 8.05×2.50 m; wb 1.78+3.11 m.

1965
Sisu (SF)
KB-45

Finnish-built 3-ton 4×4 cargo/personnel truck with various interesting features including planetary reduction gears in the wheel hubs and a hydraulic system for driving trailers. This system comprises an engine-driven oil pump and hydraulic hub motors in the wheels of the trailer or gun, providing an all-wheel drive 'train'. The engine is a British Leyland 0.400 and with optional turbo charging develops 160 bhp. It is located behind the cab.

Engine: six-in-line, diesel (Leyland), 135 bhp, 6.54 litres.
Transmission: five-speed (OD top) with two-speed transfer.
Chassis: ladder type; leaf spring suspension.
Body: cab with removable hard top, hinged windscreen and side windows; steel body with hoops and tilt.
Dimensions: 5.70×2.30 m; wb 3.40 m.

131

1965
Thornycroft (GB)
TFA/B81 'Nubian' Mk VII

The 'Nubian' chassis was produced for many years in 4×4 and 6×6 form and became very popular as a basis for fire-fighting vehicles. The vehicle shown was bodied and equipped by Pyrene Co. Ltd of Brentford and was developed for the RAF to meet the requirement for a high-performance fire crash tender. It carried a comprehensive array of equipment. The roof-mounted monitor could discharge foam at 5,000 gallons per min for 1.8 min with a throw of 95 ft (29 m).
Engine: eight-in-line, petrol (RR), 235 bhp, 6.52 litres.
Transmission: five-speed with two-speed transfer.
Chassis: ladder type; leaf spring suspension.
Body: large crew cab; rear body comprising lockers for tools and equipment, 700-gal water and 110-gal foam compound tank, etc.
Dimensions: 23 ft 10½ in×8 ft 0 in; wb (mean) 12 ft 3 in.

1966
International (AUS)
Mark V 6×6

In 1959 the Australian Army took
delivery of the first batch of the first
Australian tactical 2½-ton 4×4 truck
which had been designed and developed by International Harvester of
Australia in conjunction with the Army
Design Establishment. Pilot models of
a 5-ton 6×6 version were delivered
in 1960 and volume production of this
type commenced in 1966. With the
exception of the rear bogie and the
fitting of twin carburettors it was
basically similar to the 4×4 type.
Engine: six-in-line, petrol, 150 bhp,
4.62 litres.
Transmission: five-speed with
two-speed transfer.
Chassis: ladder type; leaf spring
suspension (inverted on rear bogie).
Body: closed steel cab; dropside
steel body with troop seats, hoops and
tilt.
Dimensions: 270×96 in;
wb (mean) 148½ in.

133

1966
Alvis (GB)
'Stalwart' Mk 2

This High-Mobility Load Carrier was a 5-ton 6×6 truck with amphibious capability, first conceived in 1959 as a private venture by Alvis on a 'Salamander' fire fighter chassis. The first models were supplied to the British Army during the early 1960s, the improved Mk 2 was made from June 1966–April 1972. Water propulsion at 6¼ mph maximum was provided by Dowty Hydrojet units.

Engine: eight-in-line, petrol (RR), 220 bhp, 6.52 litres.
Transmission: five-speed forward and reverse.
Chassis: unitary body-cum-chassis construction; independent suspension with torsion bars.
Body: watertight cab (entry through roof hatch) and steel dropside body with tilt.
Dimensions: 20 ft 10 in×8 ft 7 in; wb 5 ft 0 in+5 ft 0 in.

1966
Ford (USA)
M656

About 1960 some US truck manufacturers produced prototypes for new 3½- and 5-ton six- and eight-wheel drive high-mobility amphibious tactical trucks. Following tests, the 5-ton 8×8 configuration was chosen and a Ford-designed model, 'XM 656', was further developed and standardized as 'M656' in 1966. Ford received a series production contract in 1968 and several body types were mounted on this chassis. Shown is the cargo type with air-inflated weatherseals on doors and body sides to provide a watertight hull for swimming.

Engine: six-in-line, multi-fuel (Continental), 210 bhp, 7.83 litres.
Transmission: six-speed automatic with single-speed transfer.
Chassis: ladder type; tapered leaf spring suspension (inverted).
Body: soft-top aluminium cab; dropside aluminium cargo/personnel body with hoops and tilt.
Dimensions: 278×95½ in; wb 58+90+58 in.

1966
Tatra (ČS)
T813 'Kolos'

High-mobility 8-ton 8×8 cargo/personnel carrier and artillery prime mover of the Czechoslovakian Army. Developed during the mid-1960s it went into volume production in 1968. Its construction which incorporates a backbone chassis of tubular sections and axle differential cases bolted together makes possible the relatively easy production of other chassis configurations. Examples of such derivations are 4×4 and 6×6 prime movers and an armoured vehicle.

Engine: twelve-in-vee, diesel, air-cooled, 250 bhp, 17.64 litres.
Transmission: dual-range five-speed plus overdrive, providing 20 forward and 4 reverse ratios; permanent all-wheel drive.
Chassis: tubular backbone type; swing axles with leaf spring suspension.
Body: steel closed cab, seating seven; steel dropside body with hoops and tilt.
Dimensions: 8.80×2.50 m; wb 1.65+2.20+1.45 m.

1967
Berliet (F)
TBO15M3 6×4 HC

Basically a commercial truck this Berliet 20-ton tractor unit is used by the French Army in conjunction with a 35/45-ton Coder semi-trailer for road transportation of medium tanks such as the American 'M47 Patton' and the French 'AMX30'. Located immediately behind the cab is a double-drum winch of 2×15-ton capacity for pulling disabled tanks on to the semi-trailer.

Engine: six-in-line, diesel, 255 bhp, 14.78 litres.
Transmission: dual-range five-speed (10F2R).
Chassis: ladder type; leaf spring suspension (inverted on rear bogie).
Body: closed steel cab with three seats; fifth wheel coupling for semi-trailer.
Dimensions (tractor): 8.23×3.07 m; wb 3.74+1.52 m.

1967
EWK/KHD (D)
MCL 60 'Alligator' M2

Amphibious bridging and ferrying vehicle, produced by Eisenwerke Kaiserslautern and Klöckner-Humbolt-Deutz. The first prototypes appeared in 1963 and were developed from the French Gillois vehicle. All four wheels (with single 16.00-20 tyres) and the twin propellers are driven by a pair of Deutz engines. The unit can operate either solo or in conjunction with others to form a bridge or for ferrying loads of up to 50 tons. The equipment is used by several European armies.

Engine: twin eight-in-vee, multi-fuel, air-cooled (Deutz), 178 bhp, 12.67 litres.
Transmission: six-speed with two-speed transfer.
Chassis: integral light alloy construction with independent suspension, adjustable for height.
Body: closed cab at front, bridging ramps amidships; folding side pontoons.
Dimensions: 11.31×3.00 m; wb 5.35 m.

1968
Ural (USSR)
Ural-375D

First introduced in 1961 this range of medium 6×6 cross-country trucks came in several variants, including cargo/personnel and prime mover trucks, tractor trucks, crane trucks and chassis/cab for special applications such as rocket launchers. It was available commercially and was fitted with a special cold-starting system for use in Arctic conditions. Some military models had a soft-top cab.

Engine: eight-in-vee, petrol, 195 bhp, 7.00 litres.
Transmission: five-speed (OD top) with two-speed transfer.
Chassis: ladder type; leaf spring suspension (inverted on rear bogie).
Body: closed steel cab; cargo/personnel body with hoops and tilt.
Dimensions: 7.35×2.69 m; wb 3.50+1.40 m.

1969
Volvo (S)
4141 'Laplander'

In 1959 AB Volvo of Göteborg, Sweden, introduced prototypes for a new light cross-country vehicle with forward control. Designated 'L3314' 'Laplander' it soon went into volume production and during the 1960s considerable quantities were purchased by the Swedish and Norwegian armed forces. It was also sold for non-military use. In 1969 pilot models for modernized versions were produced, designated Series 4140. There were 4×4 (shown), 6×6 and 8×8 variants. Military trucks along similar lines were developed in Austria (Steyr-Puch) and Britain (Rover).

Engine: four-in-line, petrol, 94 bhp, 2 litres (or 3-litre 130-bhp six).
Transmission: four-speed with two-speed transfer.
Chassis: ladder type; leaf spring and rubber suspension.
Body: soft-top cab; dropside body (test body shown).
Dimensions: 4.26×1.81 m; wb 2.30 m.

1969
Barreiros (E)
6618M 'Panter'

During the early 1960s the Spanish firm of Barreiros Diesel SA (now Chrysler España SA) introduced a range of tactical forward control all-wheel drive vehicles, namely the 1½-ton 4×4 'Comando', the 2½-ton 4×4 'Panter' II and the 5-ton 6×6 'Panter' III. There was also a normal control model of the latter (shown), patterned on the US 'M-Series' 5-ton 6×6. On all models the power unit could be converted with relative ease to run on petrol or diesel fuel by changing cylinder heads, injection/ignition equipment, etc.

Engine: six-in-line, diesel, 170 bhp, 10.18 litres.

Transmission: five-speed (OD top) with two-speed transfer.

Chassis: ladder type; leaf spring suspension (inverted on rear bogie).

Body: hard-top cab; steel cargo body with hoops and tilt.

Dimensions: 6.75×2.25 m; wb 3.38+1.37 m.

1970
Bedford (GB)
MK

To supersede the standard Bedford RL 4-tonner the British Ministry of Defence tested various prototypes produced by BMC (Austin), Rootes (Commer) and Vauxhall (Bedford) to the same general specification. The latter was eventually selected and after the necessary detail modifications, entered service in 1970/71. The very un-military cab was, again, inherited from the contemporary civilian forward-control truck (TK range). Various body types may be fitted.

Engine: six-in-line, multi-fuel, 108 bhp, 5.42 litres.
Transmission: four-speed with two-speed transfer.
Chassis: ladder type; leaf spring suspension.
Body: steel closed cab; cargo body with removable sides (carrying aluminium container, suitable for various purposes).
Dimensions (truck): 259×98 in; wb 156 in.

140

1970
Mercedes-Benz (D)
LG494

This eight-wheeled all-wheel drive amphibious armoured car was developed and produced by Daimler-Benz as one of the prototypes for a new generation of tactical and armoured vehicles for use by the *Bundeswehr*. Weighing 19 tons the vehicle is of modern and sophisticated design. Other types in the same 'family' included 4×4, 6×6 and 8×8 armoured personnel carriers and a range of 4×4, 6×6 and 8×8 amphibious trucks, all with a high content of standardized components.

Engine: ten-in-vee, multi-fuel, 390 bhp (diesel), 370 bhp (petrol), 16.0 litres.
Transmission: semi-automatic.
Chassis: integral construction; two bogies of two rigid axles with coil spring suspension.
Body: armoured hull with rotating turret; crew four, including driver.
Dimensions: 7.66×2.98 m; wb 1.40+2.36+1.40 m.

1971
Saviem/Renault (F)
TP3

Typical example of French militarized commercial truck. The basic chassis was modified by fitting a driven front axle, transfer case and oversize (9.00-16) tyres, single rear. The cab was cut at waist level and fitted with hinged windscreen to fold forward as shown and a soft top. Payload capacity 1200 kg or twelve men in main body (removable bench seats in centre or along sides). Front-mounted winch optional. Also with integral all-steel van body (ambulance and mobile control room).
Engine: four-in-line, petrol, 78 bhp, 2.6 litres.
Transmission: four-speed with two-speed transfer.
Chassis: ladder type; leaf spring suspension.
Body: soft-top cab; steel body with hoops and tilt.
Dimensions: 5.00 × 2.00 m; wb 2.64 m.

142

Index